THE CREATIVE WRITING COMPASS

The Creative Writing Compass presents a dynamic navigational instrument for creative writers and those learning to be creative writers, providing a method for developing and advancing knowledge of creative writing. Award-winning novelist Graeme Harper explores the many fluid interactions of the imagination and the physical acts of writing. He includes observations and approaches that can be personalized to assist with writing decisions.

This distinctive guide to the practice of creative writing and to its critical understanding is based in the actions of creation and in each individual writer's responses to those actions. The 'compass' refers to the range of outcomes produced in creative writing – from finished works to the experiences creative writers have while writing – as well as to the range of forces, influences, and meanings that any writer is likely to encounter along the way.

The Creative Writing Compass is a guide to the consideration, progression, and completion of creative writing projects, providing ways of thinking about work-in-progress as well as ways of determining and reflecting on end results.

Graeme Harper is Professor of Creative Writing and Dean of The Honors College at Oakland University, Michigan, USA. He is Chief Editor of *New Writing: The International Journal for the Practice and Theory of Creative Writing*. An award-winning fiction writer, publishing as Brooke Biaz, his recent books are *Stimulus, Intention and Process in Creative Writing* (2024) and the novel *Releasing the Animals* (2023).

I keep hearing a wondrous echo: 'to write your novel, story, poem or film follow your own personal compass'.

Brooke Biaz

Author of the novel *Releasing the Animals* (2023)

THE CREATIVE WRITING COMPASS

Graeme Harper

 Routledge
Taylor & Francis Group

LONDON AND NEW YORK

Designed cover image: Anthony Cantin, Unsplash

First published 2025
by Routledge
4 Park Square, Milton Park, Abingdon, Oxon OX14 4RN

and by Routledge
605 Third Avenue, New York, NY 10158

Routledge is an imprint of the Taylor & Francis Group, an informa business

British Library Cataloguing-in-Publication Data
A catalogue record for this book is available from the British Library

Library of Congress Cataloging-in-Publication Data
Names: Harper, Graeme, author.
Title: The creative writing compass / Graeme Harper.
Description: Abingdon, Oxon; New York, NY: Routledge, 2024. |
Includes bibliographical references and index. |
Identifiers: LCCN 2024006851 (print) | LCCN 2024006852 (ebook) |
ISBN 9781032004938 (hardback) | ISBN 9781032004907 (paperback) |
ISBN 9781003174400 (ebook)
Subjects: LCSH: Creative writing. | Authorship.
Classification: LCC PN187 .H36493 2024 (print) |
LCC PN187 (ebook) | DDC 808.07—dc23/eng/20240325
LC record available at https://lccn.loc.gov/2024006851
LC ebook record available at https://lccn.loc.gov/2024006852

ISBN: 978-1-032-00493-8 (hbk)
ISBN: 978-1-032-00490-7 (pbk)
ISBN: 978-1-003-17440-0 (ebk)

DOI: 10.4324/9781003174400

Typeset in Sabon
by codeMantra

CONTENTS

PREFACE

'Creative writers use the alphabet,' I say to the audience. 'They use the alphabet, in an ordered but interesting way.'

The audience looks back, curious of course.

'The same alphabet,' I say, 'that other humans employ matter-of-factly to punch out a quick text to a business associate who is late for lunch, or to rattle off a spirited email to a languid colleague.'

The audience is transfixed.

'The same alphabet they might use,' I continue, 'to offer a project report to an employer or to scribble out a grocery list they then supplement with pick-ups in the candy aisle.'

I naturally pause, to savor my joke, but strangely no recognition of this joke comes back from the audience.

'Written words!' I cry out.

$$cat$$

'Ordinary *words*! Not so often words sung or presented with calligraphic artistry. Words! Put in an order. Words typed, most often. Sometimes words counted, such as in certain kinds of poetry, of course. Words pounded out. Sometimes words handwritten. Words we write but also speak. And also words we reserve mostly for writing.'

Some of the audience are fidgeting. Try as I might, I cannot help finding this disappointing. One audience member has now taken off her shoe and is pulling distractedly at her sock. I suspect it was once white. Now it is a fawn-colored lump. Inside-out, askew, and bunched up under her heel, she pulls at it distractedly. I imagine it smells like roasting corn.

'*The alphabet!*' I cry. 'Put into an imaginative order, of course!'

The shoeless young lady stops tugging her hosiery. Other fresh faces widen. '*Words!*' I shout.

A few bottom lips begin to quiver. I push on, regardless.

'Words that are known – or can be known – *by other people*. So of course the meaning of those words is shared. You know? Person to person. One of us to another of us. And those others to further others. And so on. And so on. And so forth. These are shared marvels! Exchanged oddities! Explored attitudes! Cares. *Considerations!* Observations. Loves and . . . losses. *Possibilities and purposes!*'

Miss Holtmayer suddenly appears beside me, blindingly bright in yellow, swaying a little, in a folksy dance. I imagine she spends much of each working day performing this kind of choreography.

'I *am* sorry,' she says, smiling faintly, close to my ear, 'we're going to have to stop.'

Her face reminds me of warm eggs.

'I'm sorry,' she says, still very close, 'they have nap now.' Her small mouth puckers smaller. Her eyes almost close. And then she swings back powerfully to the audience on the mats, legs crossed, some yawning, some staring up at the ceiling, some picking at their ears or noses, some with their sticky hands glued to their bare knees.

'What do we say to Mr. Harper, children?' she calls out.

The audience, crying and otherwise, bursts into a sniffling racket of 'Thank you, Mr. Harper!' that belies their tiny sizes.

So appears the me I never wanted to be. Poor kids!

Fortunately, this opening scene (and hopefully, this opening me) is fictional. Factually, unlike that guy visiting stoic Miss Holtmayer's 2nd Grade Class, I hope I'm more sensitive to banalities. That's why I would have been in two minds about calling this book *The Creative Writing Compass*, if not that I am confident in the journey and navigation analogy. It is a simple yet truthful representation of what we need to write creatively. It is apt, the way trees depicted as umbrellas is an apt metaphor, and music portrayed as medicine is an apt metaphor.

Good metaphors add layers to our human understanding, and undertaking some creative writing seems to me clearly a movement from one place to another – primarily from the non-written to the written. It is often a movement that can be described as setting off on a project; seeking guides and directions to take; going on a quest to discover or explain or record to respond to or admire or contemplate; exploring ideas or imaginative conjectures; journeying from a beginning to an end of a project; and searching in some way, however minor or major that quest might be. It is also often a movement that is layered and entwined – imagination and memory and observation and analysis and consideration and influence and attitude and feeling, all connecting and supporting and influencing each other. Suggestions on navigating techniques and tools that would assist someone navigating all this would seem to me a useful contribution to make – especially if it could be made sympathetic to the individuality of any writer's experience.

When we use a compass, we use art and we use science – because a compass is a scientific instrument that, throughout time, has been interpreted by imaginative as well as analytical minds.

In this vein, yacht designer and writer, Alan Gurney, in his book *The Compass,* speaks of 12th-century scholar-monk, Alexander Neckham, who was the first to record a magnetized metal needle being used as a marine compass (Gurney, 2004: 33) while, tellingly perhaps, otherwise spending his time writing imaginative folk tales and exploring legends.

Some historians suggest navigation began as an art but, with the invention of more sophisticated instruments, creation and accumulation of maps and charts, and ultimately the impact of advanced digital technologies, increasingly has become a science. Perhaps so!

Nevertheless, the art within navigation continues to be obvious today. Observation, contemplation, assessment, imaginative leaps, conjectures, interpretations, and beliefs are key elements of using a compass and are all reflective of both art and science.

Ultimately, even if the brilliant kids of Miss Holtmayer's class were sitting on their bright multi-colored mats only in front of my fictional evil doppelganger, I didn't feel the real, less evil me was rolling out too many chestnuts to set to work on a book called *The Creative Writing Compass.* Had I felt that way, there were other figurative models immediately on hand. In lighter moments (and in darker moments too when I was unsure I was making any progress on this book), I was half-tempted to use them. For example, living here in a northern suburb of Detroit, America's 'Motor City', I warmly pondered writing a book entitled *A Creative Writing Bucket of Bolts* or setting to work on the more energetic but odious *Revving Your Creative Writing Engine.* Either might have worked – locally, at least. Or perhaps I could have written the steely but infinitely useful tome: *Tools for Creative Writing.* I seem to recall that is an already published work – possibly written by a moonlighting Chevrolet mechanic; not so outrageously, as it happens: torque, timing, momentum, and meter all come from something of the same world view. In any case: 'It is pure poetry!'

A tired road screeches
Out the Corvette window
The sight of children waiting
For a looming yellow bus.

In my own mechanisms metaphor – incorporating a hardtop, a convertible, and possibly a lascivious pink limousine and a muscular blue pick-up truck – the miracle of art and communication that is creative writing would remind me of the industrious car fans around the Detroit suburbs. In Royal Oak or Dearborn, Lake Orion or Wyandotte, Plymouth or Birmingham, they labor nightly under their bright garage lights – signed pictures of Presley and Seger overlooking Coke machines and posters of Gumby and 'Better Made' potato chips – building and rebuilding motors and chassis, reflected in mirrors and shining panels that, by the time they roll them out onto the driveway, are transformed into gleaming examples of American ingenuity.

In that alternative book, I would go on to describe the amazement of audiences, makeshift and planned – roadside on Woodward, trackside, and lot-side too – the roar, the leather, the impossible mirror gleam of the impossible chrome (they used to make car bumpers with electroplating using hexavalent chromium on steel; now it is plastic or, more accurately, thermoplastic olefins and a reinforcing filler of calcium carbonate. The end results look different, but so is the process. Incidentally!).

I would then point out, and not to take anything away from the shine and color, the mirrors and the roaring, that this is only an indication of those long silent nights in the grease shop, not an embodiment of them. So it goes with creative writing.

Metaphors deepen our knowledge and stimulate our greater understanding. They are mental tools for formulating our ideas when we're not quite at the explaining stage, and they help us explain when we reach that stage.

I am drawn to the compass metaphor, and the navigation, explorations and journeys, movement, quests, tracks, starting points, destinations, and points of arrival it contains. Other creative writers are drawn to similar metaphors, comparisons, and allusions. For example, 2020 Nobel Literature Laureate, Louise Glück says, 'when I'm trying to put a poem or a book together, I feel like a tracker in the forest following a scent, tracking only step to step' (Glück, 2014: 2). Whether they are mental or physical, the tools and instruments we use for creative writing matter. That said, there remains something disturbing about the idea of entirely mechanical creative writing. Automated creative writing feels contradictory, primarily because the human empathy of the act and actions of creative writing is far more essential to us than the material presence of the finished results – and it long has been.

For instance, when in 1913 French mathematician Émile Borel published what became known as the 'infinite monkey theorem', in which he proposed that a monkey hitting typewriter keys at random for an infinite amount of time would eventually type a recognizable text, what was most alarming was that this text could be a work by William Shakespeare. In fact, the infinite monkey theorem pointed toward the suggestion that a monkey would eventually write the *entire* works of Shakespeare! That notion was considered simultaneously possible and antithetical to the nature of creative writing.

Creative writing is imbued with active human intent and personal feeling and in this represents something meaningful if intangible about ourselves. It is often something we also share with others. Entirely automated writing might be acceptable, even valuable, if it is solely informational – not least for the efficiency of its creation, its ability to draw on vast amounts of knowledge recorded and stored out in the world. That is incredibly useful, as long as we can trust the automation algorithm that creates and reviews that information, of course, and likewise that drafts that kind of writing. But creative writing is different.

Fundamentally, creative writing needs humans involved at the core of the effort, generating and producing both the successes and the failures of that effort, engaging in the struggles as well as the triumphs. The actions need to be ours, and the results of those actions are only one part of this writing story.

In the early 20th century, in the Detroit suburb of Highland Park, once a small rural village and later an industrial hot spot, Henry Ford introduced the moving assembly line. The goal was to produce sturdy, inexpensive automobiles; and, not much more than ten years later, ten million of those had already rolled off the line. This was not quite the embodiment of the infinite monkey theorem for automobile production, because it involved varied tasks, human input determining these tasks, and stations on the line where humans did these tasks. But the moving assembly line nevertheless did produce sameness and did involve repetition. It soon became both a symbol of progress and a warning of the potential dangers of mechanization – portrayed around twenty years later in Charlie Chaplin's satirical film *Modern Times* (1936). Twenty more years and robots were already taking over many of the old assembly line tasks, with humans working to inspect rather than assemble, spending time on tasks requiring the kinds of dexterity robots could not yet achieve, and the kinds of open-thinking robots could not yet emulate.

By the early 21st century, artificial intelligence was as much a part of the working lives of ordinary humans as it was, people knew, still an assortment of nascent inventions. Again, the cinema had already shown popular concern through such films as *2001: A Space Odyssey* (Kubrick, 1968), *The Terminator* (Cameron, 1984), and *Avengers: Age of Ultron* (Whedon, 2015). The challenge to free, creative, empathetic humans will underpin and inform that concern.

Creative writing is a celebration of human free will. We exemplify the humanity in our writing choices (whether choices of subject and theme or technical writerly choices of structure, style, and tone). Entirely identical works are neither our goal nor our preference. It is not the aspects of assembly that attract us; rather, it is the humanity that brings about those aspects. In the actions of creative writing, it is not often the efficiency of the work at hand – in fact, sometimes it is quite the opposite. We express degrees of skepticism at creative writing done too quickly, thoughts and ideas in it too little dwelt upon, conjectures too offhandedly explored, emotions too fleetingly expressed. These are seen as opportunities missed. There is no moving belt here to take us inevitably from one station of action and then on to another, no singular route to follow from initial inspiration to final creative work. This is an odyssey rather than an assembly line, an undertaking that could just as appreciably be meandering rather than direct.

So, if creative writing involves the assembling of lines of writing on a screen or page, in some way, then it is work that both moves forward toward some final completed thing and work that requires the assembling to reflect our ongoing, resilient belief in our human selves. The intelligence applied cannot be artificial, and it involves insightful acts of mental and emotional dexterity that are not replicable in the non-human world. Occasionally, someone attempts to challenge readers to determine if a particular new poem or story was written by a human or entirely by a machine. Sometimes a reader finds it hard to tell. The salient question is: why does it matter? In the answer to that question lies the reason we value the work of creative writers.

I first conceived of this book one afternoon, just over four years ago. For those with chimerical inclinations, imagine a windswept cliff top, a vast ocean, a small, distant silhouette perched on the cliff edge, looking out to sea. . . . I more or less then started writing. A bit more, a bit less, depending on where you believe writing starts – in the physical appearance of writing 'on the page' *or* in the thoughts and feelings we have about a writing project.

That night, I sent myself some emails with a handful of points about what I thought the book would do; tried a few paragraphs; over a matter of weeks filled up a few pages, widely spaced; began a book proposal that aimed to

take those thoughts to a potential conclusion; sent myself some emails as if me talking to me electronically was entirely ordinary; wrote impromptu, and often at inconvenient moments, on scraps of paper, in the middle of the night on a notepad by my bed, on backs of bills and fronts of other people's memos; finally finished and soon after submitted the book proposal; created a title page and toyed with the initial list of chapters, changing the list already; awaited the proposal's review; emailed; scribbled; thought; wrote some fiction, half a new story that went nowhere and a full draft of one that did; sent an email to myself with the title of a potential novel as the subject line, and nothing more; received reviews of the proposal. Soon after, I signed the contract to write this book. Other books were then completed before this one. In between completing those books, I wrote some draft sections of *The Creative Writing Compass*. I set off heeding the now final title, which worked for me for a while, but I wasn't sure of it in those earlier drafts. So I tried other titles, beginning with *Navigating Creative Writing*. This worked – at least for a while. Ultimately, it seemed too lacking in direction, strangely, as if we each (me, the reader) were attempting something potentially circular, or as a way of getting around something rather than moving forward. It also seemed a smidgen too nautical. At one point, about six months into writing the book, I renamed it *A Complete Atlas of Creative Writing* – on which, very shortly afterwards, the fiction-writer Brooke Biaz commented: 'Reminds me of a 5th grade Geography textbook'. Too true! So, then I came up with a title with the word *Directions* in it, which certainly was directional if entirely empty of real character (so much so that I now forget the full abandoned title!). Someone tells you directions, you're either obliged to follow them or to make up excuses for rejecting them ('The guy hasn't a clue – did you see the color of his shoes?'). So, none of the alternative titles got to the crux of the metaphor, or of the idea, or the contribution I was trying to make.

In all this, I was ardently grasping for titles to guide my own navigation of writing this book – which brings to mind how funny it is that the obvious is not always that obvious. That was another motivation for writing this book.

I later added and then subtracted the subtitle *Explorations*, wondering if a reminder was needed (to me, perhaps, mostly) of the exploratory reasoning, emotional responses, now and then self-awareness, considerable critical thinking, and creativity that we each draw upon when writing creatively. Ultimately, I decided that human exploration was self-evident in creative writing.

Writing projects often emerge when others are already in motion and shift as ideas become more formed, and your imagination, in one or more of its organizational, speculative, combinatory modes, informs and influences the choices you make. Sometimes one project then leapfrogs others. Sometimes a project waits on the sidelines. Sometimes it disappears and is not missed, or it is returned to well beyond when it is conceived, and with some degree of interest, and then fails to excite, and therefore never happens. Writing is like that for so many writers. It is not always linear. It is very often a mosaic.

I have had time to live with the compass as a guiding concept for this book, and to test it further through my own creative writing practice, to explore it when talking with other creative writers, even if I did not mention it by name to Brooke and the others, to read around some more, including numerous articles arriving at *New Writing: The International Journal for the Practice and Theory of Creative Writing* (Routledge), which I edit, and to think some more. The basic idea around compass navigation emerged out of an appetite for writing an alternative creative writing 'how to' book. That idea continues to animate me and to feel significant.

A number of us involved in creative writing around universities have critically examined the approach taken, historically, in creative writing 'how to' books. Unquestionably, these books have been a staple of popular publishing about creative writing. Books in this vein don't all have 'How to' in their titles, but the genre is recognizable and there are indeed numerous unambiguously titled examples of it, such as *How to Write a Novel* and *How to Write Poetry*. The declared purpose of these books, other than the legitimate but not always so openly declared purpose of making someone some money, is to teach the reader about how to write creatively. Specifically, to teach those who purchase these books something practical about creative writing. This practical emphasis has not in itself been the focus of objections. Rather, the focus of objections has been on whether what is said in these books provides enough of a sense, or even an accurate sense of how creative writing is done.

Creative writing is unique in its primary use of written words for the purposes of both art and communication. How this is done is intersectional and layered, physical and incorporeal, transformative and ordinary, contemplative and speculative. It cannot be glossed by focusing mostly on visible literary structures or the conspicuous systemic characteristics of writing styles, forms, or genres that are shared between writers and their audiences. It cannot be understood by saying creative writing is ultimately mysterious, transcending ordinariness, and that it is largely located in personal psychology and personal history and therefore is impossible to truly reach – except by doing it and, even then, without entirely knowing what you are doing or how you are doing what you are doing. In reality, creative writing needs to be approached as many actions, thoughts, feelings, expectations, and results – happening all at once.

It is the intersecting, layered, conversational character of creative writing that defines and determines it, along with the individuality you bring to it as a writer, and the communicative origins of it, beyond yourself. Navigating all this is entirely possible, and frequently exhilarating – if, of course, you have some kind of metaphoric compass to assist.

A map is not the actual territory to which it refers, but it is an attempt to symbolize that territory. A map needs to be read to be used. The sound of a bell doesn't present a grave danger, but it might indicate the presence of one. We decide if it does or does not, and we act accordingly. Maps, bells, the stars, radar, GPS, lighthouses, whistles, depth sounders, sextants, signal lamps, and flags, all these have informed human navigation, but they are not the navigation itself. That is the thought that struck me when thinking 'how to' go about creative writing.

A compass points north; but, it doesn't take you anywhere, without you taking action to travel. Using a compass is a specific sort of wayfinding. It is about determining positions, about finding routes, and about following them. It is about orientating yourself and about making decisions. A personal compass can help us do all these things. That is the sort of book about creative writing I thought would be worthwhile writing. *The Creative Writing Compass* is that book. Ultimately, choosing to travel is up to us.

London
July 2023
Rochester, Michigan
January 2024

Bibliography

Borel, Émile, 'La mécanique statique et l'irréversibilité' ('Statistical Mechanics and Irreversibility'), *Journal of Physics: Theories and Application*, 3, no. 1, 1913, pp. 189–196.

Cameron, James, *The Terminator*, Los Angeles: Hemdale Pacific Western Productions, 1984.

Glück, Louise in William Giraldi, 'Internal Tapestries: A Q&A With Louise Glück', *Poets and Writers Magazine*, September/October 2014.

Gurney, Alan, *The Compass*, New York: Norton, 2004.

Kubrick, Stanley, *2001: A Space Odyssey*, London: Stanley Kubrick Productions, 1968.

Whedon, Joss, *Avengers: Age of Ultron*, Burbank: Marvel Studios, 2015.

1

STARTING

When I began I had no idea of the way ahead. I wished only to do a book.
(Naipaul, 2007: 80)

V.S. Naipaul, who had 'no idea of the way ahead', and 'wished only to do a book', went on to write over 30 books, around half of them works of fiction. In 2001, he was awarded the Nobel Prize in literature. In announcing the award, the Swedish Academy described him as 'a literary circumnavigator, only ever really at home in himself, in his inimitable voice' (Swedish Academy). A certain kind of navigator, then, as much emotionally and psychologically as he might have been in the geographic world.

How do we each set out on a creative writing project so that we can identify directions and ways of going forward successfully? What is the nature and focus of creative writers early drafting, before they revise or begin to edit, their initial sense of a project's direction, their perceived aims and objectives, their understanding of the nature, and motivation behind their passion and commitment to a creative writing project?

To answer these questions, we creative writers become orientated: we get to know what creative writing is (in general, and in relation to any given ideas and ideals in our society and that we hold individually), along with what ways creative writing comes about – what combination of thinking, and action, and imagining takes place to make creative writing happen. We discover how someone can go about creative writing not only as something confirmed and made valid by its final results (the story, poem, novel, we

DOI: 10.4324/9781003174400-1

produce) but as an activity that evolves in and during the practice, so that directions we take can both define and refine our goal setting and be considered part of the overall experience.

When starting out on creative writing, we are beginning a journey of discovery and invention that is distinctive in the writing world in its heightening of newness and imaginativeness and variety. Analogously, starting is defined in a variety of ways. Many of the most basic dictionary definitions provide semantic variations on a theme that shows an interest in creatively interpreting what starting anything might entail. For example, 'if you start to do something, you do something that you were not doing before and you continue doing it' (Collins) and 'to come into being, activity, or operation' (Merriam-Webster).

These basic definitions also include meanings such as 'when something starts, or if someone starts it, it takes place from a particular time' (Collins), and 'if you start an engine, car, or machine, or if it starts, it begins to work' (Collins). Others include 'to do the first part of something' (Britannia) and 'the action or an act of starting to move, originally at the beginning of a race, later of any journey' (Oxford).

It is suggested that 'if you start by doing something, or if you start with something, you do that thing first in a series of actions' (Collins). Eighteenth-century English man of letters and lexicographer Samuel Johnson records in his famous dictionary that starting involves 'a sudden rousing to action; excitement' (Johnson), while renowned American lexicographer, Noah Webster, notes in his 1828 dictionary that starting is 'to bring into motion; to produce suddenly to view or notice' (Webster).

Any or all of these definitions – whether starting as 'doing something you were not doing before' or 'first in a series of actions' or beginning 'to work' or any of the others – might be the influence on our thinking of how we start some creative writing. These definitions relate multiple elements, rather than magnifying a sole element of what it means to start creative writing. All of them or any of them can be most correct for one creative writer or for another. In some way, they are, of course, all generally correct, because there is no single way of starting out on a writing project. Even semantically our starting is unfixed.

Nonetheless, we are reminded throughout literary history that starting creative writing does involve some form of 'putting pen to paper'. Says 1949 Nobel laureate in Literature William Faulkner: 'Get it down. Take chances. It may be bad, but it's the only way you can do anything really good' (Faulkner, quoted in Messud, 1997). For Celine Song, writer and director of the multi-award-winning film *Past Lives* (2023) 'it usually starts in my Notes app on the phone' (Song, 2023). In their classroom research study of children's motivation to write, Caroline Barratt-Pugh, Amelia Ruscoe, and Janet Fellowes report:

All four teachers made a deliberate decision to focus on meaning when providing feedback, with positive results:

> I've stopped correcting their work. I have started having conversations with them. . . and what actually happened was the children realised I respected their work. . . They started writing more, they started writing all over the classroom.
>
> *(Barratt-Pugh et al., 2021: 223)*

As with these examples, much written historically about creative writing focuses on this putting pen to paper (in whatever fashion this is done). There is good reason for this: like all writing, creative writing is the inscribing of words to make them more durable and transportable, from place to place, and over time. Walter Stevens goes further than this when he says: 'the actual or "true" history of writing is a long and still incomplete story of technology – a history of signs, the instruments used to inscribe them, and the practical possibilities for interpreting them' (Stevens, 2023: 18). True enough. What is highlighted and elevated in *creative* writing is always that while inscribing is instrumental to doing it inscribing is only some of what occurs. That is, we can't write creatively without inscribing words in some way, but the feeling, and thinking, and imagining that take place are significant too. It might be you begin your 'series of actions' (as the definition goes) well before you put pen to paper, and that this takes place at a particular time and it is something you were not doing before'. This is very far from mechanical, it is a relational natural practice involving our minds and our bodies. Irish poet Seamus Heaney, in his 1966 poem 'Digging', exploring his own writing labor in relation to the farming labor of his father and grandfather, begins:

> Between my finger and my thumb
> The squat pen rests; snug as a gun.
>
> Under my window, a clean rasping sound
> When the spade sinks into gravelly ground:
> My father, digging. I look down
>
> (Heaney, 1991: 13)

Heaney records elsewhere that, for him, the physical action of writing is preceded by the work of the mind:

> By the time you start to compose, more than half the work has been done. The crucial part of the business is what happens before you face the empty

page — the moment of first connection, when an image or a memory comes suddenly to mind and you feel the lure of the poem-life in it.

(Heaney, 2006)

Each of us arrives at our start of creative writing with territory covered and territory in need of covering. Occasionally, we can be surprised or fearful of what lies ahead. Creative writing is an emotionally engaging activity, so the practicalities of doing it are not without sometimes heightened feelings about what we each might encounter when we do it. The territory already covered when we start writing might be associated generally with life – the knowledge, and sentiments, and experiences, and observations that have gotten us to this time and place. In that regard, there is, of course, no ideal day of the week, month of the year, or year of life to start to writing creatively, and no research that shows that creative writers can only draw on specific experiences or certain forms of education, and that we all need to stop writing at a certain point in life.

Therefore, while first time novelists can be young, poets artistic, memoirists well-traveled or eclectically experienced, and screenwriters gaming geeks who are now applying their once distracted minds to writing the next Hollywood blockbuster, these are not archetypes. Creative writers can be anyone.

For all that, whether every person has equal access to the methods of exploring and making creative works is a significant question. Types of biases, cultural histories, and social and economic conditions all impact how likely it is that we each will have the opportunity to write creatively. And yet, despite all the conditions that influence access to writing, it is true to say that in literate societies the majority of people do, at the minimum, learn to write – and they do so somewhere in their early years of life.

When we are children, we are often introduced with enthusiasm to writing *creatively*. Creative writing is presented as being of wide human significance, lauded for its cultural importance and personal expressive value. Those who are successful at it – often based on the popularity of works they write, distributed as books or seen as movies or television, or games or plays, heard as music, and so on – these people are admired. It is worth remembering that this admiration is not often about the actions of creative writing themselves; rather, it is largely based in the reception of the results of those actions. It can be daunting to imagine that when we start any writing project we are participating in an activity steeped in cultural esteem and veneration – even when we personally are not the ones held in esteem or being venerated. The baggage of engaging in such a significant human activity can be weighty. However, most of what creative writers do – whether beginning, unknown writers, or experienced, revered writers – occurs out of public view in what is frequently a highly individualized and private place. This is one reason why published writers' diaries, letters, and memoirs are so popular: because they purport to offer a glimpse into a hidden world where the artistry of writing has occurred.

The question of where the orientation for any kind of journey from start to finish of a creative writing project comes with an expectation that we are all in some fashion already orientated.

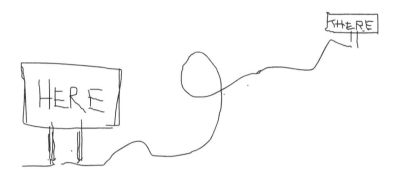

We know what words are, even if (for example) those who are sight- or hearing-impaired haven't perhaps seen or heard them in the same way the majority of others have. We know about the results of creative writing – the books, the video games, the poems, the films, the stories told in journals online and otherwise – even if these things were not seen in our childhood homes; and, even if, now, not everyone in our immediate circle embraces similar or connected interests in cultural activities, or specifically in written or broadly artistic things.

Our creative writing journey begins with the following elements. These form the basis of what I will call 'your compass'. Your compass is the sense and the actions that will help you with navigation and orientation through your creative writing, help you to start and guide your writing progress.

Who are you? Personal history, and circumstances, and psychology are primary influences on creative writing. Writers are often revered for their distinctiveness – the things they bring to their projects borne on their individual backgrounds and thought processes. But, because creative writing is such a varied practice, bound in the system and structures of writing, but unbound in being situated in the elastic and formative work of the imagination and the analytical work of written expression, the question of singular character and individual knowledge play a substantial role. For example, it is one thing to understand how written language works but another to have the creative ability to build from an observation or feeling a written work that ingeniously captures what has been seen or felt. In this way, one of the most challenging aspects of orientating any creative writing is to understand who is doing it (especially if it is you who is writing).

Sigmund Freud's well-known 1907 talk *Der Dichter und das Phantasieren* (Creative Writers and Day-Dreaming), published in 1908, is just one of a considerable number of explorations of where we creative writers get our material, if not about how we practically go about writing about it. In his 1907 talk, Freud muses:

> And now for the creative writer. May we really attempt to compare the imaginative writer with the "dreamer in broad daylight," and his creations with day-dreams? Here we must begin by making an initial distinction. We must separate writers who, like the ancient authors of epics and tragedies, take over their material ready-made, from writers who seem to originate their own material. We will keep to the latter kind, and, for the purposes of our comparison, we will choose not the writers most highly esteemed by the critics, but the less pretentious authors of novels, romances and short stories, who nevertheless have the widest and most eager circle of readers of both sexes. One feature above all cannot fail to strike us about the creations of these story-writers: each of them has a hero who is the centre of interest, for whom the writer tries to win our sympathy by every possible means and whom he seems to place under the protection of a special Providence.
>
> *(Freud, 1953: 425)*

Here Freud is attempting to locate the creative writer somewhere in relation to the material they draw upon – categorizing this in terms of where the material is found and the originality of the work undertaken. Interestingly, Freud also differentiates the 'pretentious' from the widely read – suggesting that it is the critical reception as much as the individual creation he is using to determine who those writers happen to be. Clearly this fuses two aspects: the role of the critic/reader and the activity of the writer.

Starting out, we might be aware of how certain works of creative writing have been received by professional critics and general readers, but this is only part of a greater range of considerations, not as Freud suggests a solely defining factor. Considering creative writing by others, similarly, Freud's analysis is after the fact, it is not about creative writing itself. Alternatively, we are thinking in this book of the writerly actions we undertake *when they are undertaken*-not only after they are undertaken and are understood primarily in completed works. We might not ever truly know exactly who we are, to have such a level of complete self-awareness – but if we are writing creatively we are setting off both on the basis of our individual understanding and, often frequently, on a journey of discovery that will offer confirmations or challenges, cause us to consider or reconsider sensibilities, reactions or ideas, perhaps increase our awareness, and position what we are doing in relation to who we are and why we are doing it.

What do you want to achieve with creative writing? Your metaphoric creative writing compass has a needle pointed toward a personal north. That is, unlike the magnetic north pole, a compass in this sense has an orientating mechanism oftentimes that you define. No doubt it would warrant a moment of celebration should you produce a poem that is widely agreed to be literary achievement. However, if you had been seeking to write a screenplay then the achievement might feel ironic and possibly even underwhelming – to you, at least. The novelist contracted by the publisher of their first novel to write their second one, and who then produces a short story, has something of an issue, even if they are thrilled by what they have written.

What you aim to achieve sets things in motion, and in large part determines how you view success and failure in your journey. External forces – influences of friends or family, journal deadlines, work for creative writing courses, contracts for books, editor expectations – these all potentially exert degrees of influence over your sense of achievement. Ultimately, however, that sense will be largely self-defined. The novelist who completed a brilliant short story but not (yet) the second novel they were expected to deliver might feel guilty for not delivering, but if they believe their new short story to be a terrific piece of work they might also feel content. Creative writing, which sometimes is driven by external needs and demands, is always related to the desires of the creative writer.

How do you orientate yourself to time, place, and circumstances? Contextual understanding determines a creative writer's reason for writing. It determines a lot of other things too. Creative writing is not unique in this respect; but, the main consideration for us as creative writers (and for any creative writers whose writing practice we might examine) is the relation between our orientation and the writing we are about to undertake or are undertaking. What stimuli are occurring in the wider world? What in our more immediate social or work circles? What local events, what international ones? We can ground art and communication in its moment – and look back on when and where pieces of writing were produced with an eye to the influences that are reflected in the works produced. But when endeavoring to consider this from an active creative writing point of view we're also thinking about degrees of influence and types and strength of writerly response. Simply, the combination of personal and public circumstances orientates a creative writer – and no two writers will do this in entirely the same way. The dynamic here is the product of specific responses and the strength of those external stimuli.

Orientation for a writer means psychological and physical reflexes that occur during writing and are seen (only partly) in the written work that emerges. The orientation is deeper than the text that is released into the world: the relationship between themes and subjects chosen, the direct references but also the indirect underpinnings of how a piece of work is being structured or how a thought and an imaginative leap respond to what is around us. Writing etches into place, but our intellects and our imaginations are dynamic – and these can't be fixed still, but they can be considered when we are wondering about how we orientate our writing selves. Finally, circumstances are not only stimuli they are shaping agents, metaphoric as well as literal determinants of ideas, and attitudes, and speculations. They are relational, but not only to the writing that is happening but to themselves – so time, place, and circumstances are shaping our orientation to what we are writing, how we are writing it, the direction it is taking, and ultimately the results produced.

> About the use of words, I agree, said Joyce. I know when I was writing *Ulysses* I tried to give the colour and tone of Dublin with my words; the drab, yet glistening atmosphere of Dublin, its hallucinatory vapours, its tattered confusion, the atmosphere of its bars, its social immobility – they could only be conveyed by the texture of my words.
>
> *(Power, quoting Joyce, 1974: 98)*

What is your mode of engagement with creative writing? Someone given an assignment to complete in a creative writing class has one simple, sometimes pressing, mode of engagement with creative writing. We can call this an 'imperative' mode. The logical contrast would be with a 'non-imperative' mode; for example, casually thinking you might write a poem. We're signed up to do a creative writing course, the requirement is to complete a piece or pieces of creative writing, and our intention is to finish the course – thus the imperative. Alternatively, the casual poet might want to write a poem to express an emotion, capture a thought or record something they have seen. The motivation could be strong, but it is different to that of the writer in the creative writing class; more internalized, perhaps, more self-directed, and the success more self-defined. We could think of this imperative of engagement in terms of genre too, with the collaborative nature of a screenplay or a stage play determining more of a writer's sense of others involvement in the composition of the final work than, say, a work of poetry or fiction, where most writers work individually toward their final results.

A mode of engagement can also be considered from the point of view of knowledge. The experienced creative writer can draw on previous creative writing experiences, begin work on their piece of writing in ways that are familiar, and take on board previous results when assessing progress. A less experienced creative writer might act more from other non-creative writing experiences, or draw on some kind of analogical situation (for example, the beginning writer who starts a story the way they remember one being read to them as a child) or find their orientation in a word or phrase or expression that seems to capture the essence of their idea or feeling.

So, a mode of engagement with creative writing can be familiar or un-familiar. It can be confident or apprehensive – and not necessarily because of experience, perhaps because of uncertainty about the theme or subject, perhaps because of external influences undermining self-confidence. A mode of engagement with creative writing can be related to emotions or to intel-ligence, to the instinctual as well as the planned. It can be related mostly to perceptions or to observations. A mode is a manner of doing something, a way of doing something, and in orientating ourselves to creative writing there is no generic universal mode – rather, the mode or modes we use are our own. For this reason, our mode of engagement with creative writing is a combination of our psychology and of practicality. We choose responses to our particular aspiration to write creatively. Fundamentally, we have al-ready chosen writing as our mode of artistic expression. We could have chosen to write in another way, or chosen to make some other kind of art, or chosen to speak instead of write. Children's writer Betsy Byars:

> Although I started my writing career on a manual typewriter (on my kitchen table) and now use a computer (in my studio), my actual method of writing has not changed. I write as fast as I can because until I see what I've done in print, I can't tell what's wrong with it or – hopefully – what's right about it. . .
>
> I rely a great deal on instinct. If my instinct tells me there is some-thing wrong with a manuscript, it generally is. And I will rewrite an entire manuscript – as many times as it takes – to get it right. I have also had a series of excellent editors who have helped me when my instinct failed.
>
> *(Byars, 1995: 112)*

How we set off – orientating ourselves to our choice and the modes of en-gagement with it – is an important element of understanding our creative writing. This setting off comes with its own tempo and pace, rhythm, and style of engagement (whether it is consistent or sporadic; focused or wan-dering). This can change along the way through a writing project but being aware of our mode of engagement (or modes, as often is the case) allows us to be more confident in how we are progressing, why, and to have some idea (if not always a complete idea) of where we are heading.

How much time and energy (or overall effort) can be applied? There is no universal formula scribbled something like this:

$$X \text{ (Amount of time and effort)} = Y \text{ (Results in creative writing)}$$

Many of us might prefer it to be this simple!

Personal admiration, cultural appreciation, reverence for Literature – it is easy to see why we have expectations about the effort applied to creative writing and why, colloquially, it is more surprising than expected when someone completes a writing project whose results we admire but does so with limited effort and in quick time. We expect effort, because we value the results; and we perceive a length of time will be spent, because we don't imagine anything that is this worthwhile can be done that swiftly. It is not from consistent evidence that we have come up with these ideas; but, rather, from traditional ways in which the writing arts are valued.

Interestingly, over time we have developed technological tools that have reduced the physical labor of writing – whether we consider this from the era of the quill, the dip pen, or the ballpoint pen, or from the more modern era of computing, the cell phone, and language modeling artificial intelligence. Like all tools, writing tools have been designed to reduce effort to get our projected results and, with the impact of artificial intelligence, even reduce the amount of time it takes to combine idea and thought and sentiment into some kind of simulation of a human response. Notably, the physical labor of creative writing has always been entwined with the active labor and energy of the imagination. We orientate ourselves to this kind of writing not only by relation to the means of making it, but also by artistry, combining inventiveness, newness, ingenuity, and originality.

The time and energy in these things are not only physical, and we see evidence of what we might call an 'internal orientating' as our imaginations combine memory and immediate stimuli, knowledge of what is with speculations on what might be, the day to day elements of using written words to communicate with the projections that creativity entails, the perceptions and the suppositions. This is acknowledged when creative writing classes in schools and colleges provide for students to have occasion to contemplate, and to seek out stimuli. The time and energy in such activities can't really be reduced to physical actions, but they are equally important as those actions.

Your orientation. In orientating yourself to your creative writing you have, then, a range of elements that inform how you begin and that continue to influence you in a variety of ways while you are writing. Ultimately, if you keep going, you will reach a destination of some kind. This truism actually does contain something important. That is, that creative writing involves movement toward a point where you stop doing it. That point, for many of us, is the finished novel, the poem, the script, the story. . . To reach that point, we need to seek to understand the nature, and style, and components, and dynamics of the instrument that guides us (taking instrument here to indeed mean, metaphorically, a 'compass'). And yet – and this is something we can explore further – metaphorically speaking, a compass is an instrument to aid navigation, but it is not the navigation itself, and it is certainly not the steps we have to take, the actions we have to do, and the idea and vision of where we want to reach. All that is up to us.

References

Barratt-Pugh, Caroline, Amelia Ruscoe and Janet Fellowes 'Motivation to Write: Conversations with Emergent Writers', *Early Childhood Education Journal*, 49, 2021, pp. 223–234.

Britannia, https://www.britannica.com/dictionary/start (Last Accessed, January 2, 2024).

Byars, Betsy, *Children's Books and Their Creators*, Anita Silvey (ed), Boston, MA: Houghton Mifflin, 1995.

Collins Dictionary, https://www.collinsdictionary.com/us/dictionary/english/start (Last Accessed, November 1, 2023).

Freud, Sigmund, 'Creative Writing and Daydreaming', *Collected. Papers, Vol. 4*, London: Bask Books (Hogarth Press), 1953.

Heaney, Seamus, quoted in O'Driscoll D., 'Pickings and Choosings', *The Poetry Ireland Review*, no. 87, August 2006, pp. 113–119.

Heaney, Seamus, 'Digging', *Death of a Naturalist*, Boston: Faber and Faber, 1991 (first published 1966).

Johnson, Samuel, *Samuel Johnson's Dictionary*, https://johnsonsdictionaryonline.com/views/search.php?term=start (Last Accessed, January 5, 2024).

Messud, Clare, 'Bard of the Bayou', *The Guardian*, September 20, 1997. https://www.theguardian.com/books/1997/sep/20/fiction.williamfaulkner (Last Accessed, January 4, 2024).

Naipaul, V.S., 'Two Worlds' in *Nobel Prize Lectures: From the Literature Laureates, 1986–2006*, New York: New Press, 2007.

Oxford English Dictionary, https://www.oed.com/dictionary/start_n2?tab=meaning_and_use#20875761 (Last Accessed, January 2, 2024).

Power, Arthur, *Conversations with James Joyce*, Clive Hart (ed), London: Millington, 1974.

Song, Celine in Scott Feinberg, 'I Want to Do More Than Drive the Plot Forward', *Hollywood Reporter*, 429, no. 34, 2023, pp. 80–85.

Stevens, Walter, *How Writing Made Us Human, 3000BC to Now*, Baltimore: Johns Hopkins University Press, 2023.

Swedish Academy, 'The Nobel Prize in Literature Press Release', October 11, 2001. https://www.nobelprize.org/prizes/literature/2001/press-release/ (Last Accessed, January 12, 2024).

Webster, Noah, *American Dictionary of the English Language*, 1828, https://webstersdictionary1828.com/Dictionary/start (Last Accessed, January 2, 2024).

2

THE QUEST

Heading Forward

By its nature, creative writing is both a venture and an adventure. For many of us that makes it as exciting as it is challenging. To *venture* is to dare or risk the loss of something. To *adventure* is to set out, to proceed, to explore, to challenge expectations. We venture out into the cold, perhaps. But we 'go on an adventure'. We speak of the world's adventurers with awe and admiration; but we know that venture capitalists' are often essential financial dynamos needed to accomplish a large-scale business project. The former is aspirational and ambitious and seems to challenge ordinariness; the latter is risk-taking, sometimes essential, and suggests a calculation has been made. It was from around the 1600s that venture became associated with daring and presumption, and adventure became increasingly associated with the exciting and the remarkable. Here's one story of an adventurer and writer, Dame Freya Madeline Stark (1893–1993):

> Stark had a specific goal in mind: she wanted to travel the Valley of the Assassins, a region no other European had ever explored. Accompanied by a local guide and a pack mule, she set off for the valley with the intention of conducting geographical and archaeological studies. Along the way, Stark contracted malaria, dengue fever, and dysentery, but she carried on. Upon completing her studies, Stark returned to Baghdad and then London, where she was lauded for her achievements and began writing the first of what would be many books: *The Valley of the Assassins and Other Persian Tales*.
>
> *(Grogan, 2020: 236)*

DOI: 10.4324/9781003174400-2

Not all our challenging of expectations and exploring fits the extraordinary Dame Freya model of the adventurous! Day to day, we navigate creative writing by being alert to change, and we compare assumptions and predictions with that which emerges as we write – fluidly – in a combination of both venture and adventure. Joseph Brodsky, 1991 United States Poet Laureate, writes:

> One who writes a poem writes it because the language prompts, or simply dictates, the next line. Beginning a poem, the poet as a rule doesn't know the way it's going to come out, and at times is surprised by the way it turns out, since often it turns out better than he expected, often his thought carries further than he reckoned.
>
> *(Brodsky, 2007: 267)*

Our comparative action can be focused on sensations, ideas, and principles as much as (or rather than) on the content of a piece of writing. We sometimes refer to this in a colloquial sense as 'writing your way into' something, as if somehow the fact of writing creatively has recreated *us* as much as us creating a work of poetry, fiction, or script.

Is this an empowering suggestion, or is it a disconcerting one? Possibly it is both.

Whereas in other forms of writing the venture is largely to get down 'on paper' what we know, have discovered, or wish to convey, in creative writing the added *ad*venture is to allow the act of writing itself to unearth what it is that you think or feel.

Venture-Adventure

The characteristics of a VENTURE into creative writing look like this:

Defying or challenging in some way – because creativity involves newness and invention. So, for example, the most straightforward way to relate a thought, observation or feeling would surely be just to describe it. However, creative writing has long been employed to add depth and breadth and greater intimacy between writer and audience by challenging otherwise straightforward reporting, whether at the delicate level of the variations and tonal qualities of word choice, or rhythm, or voice, or the capacious level of genre, or over-arching metaphor, or defining formal structure.

Boldness. It is a bold notion that someone might combine their own imaginative conjectures, thoughts, and observations into a communication designed to entertain, provoke thought, evoke pleasure or pain, joy or sorrow; that we might use the relatively regular medium of printed letters, inscribed expressions, to create an artistic work.

The boldness of choosing to write creatively manifests itself in individual ways while sometimes revealing the support of family or friends. For example, here in the recollection of how English novelist, Jane Austen (1775–1817) went about her creative writing:

> Jane, with her light household duties, was not only shielded and favoured by Cassandra [Austen] and Martha [Lloyd] but actively helped by their critical opinions and at least by Cassandra's willingness to argue over details in a story. The fact that Jane's novels had begun to win public admiration could only have confirmed in the eyes of her companions the rightness and worth of her labours; and if the cottage attracted too many family visitors, it was otherwise a good place for uninterrupted work. In an atmosphere in which others kept at their duties one did not have to apologize for being busy with a manuscript, and with indulgent companions one had a sense of being valued with a respectful indulgence. Here Jane Austen's mild peculiarities – her private laughter, absence of mind, obsessive enquiries into factual details, or her wish to conceal her novel-writing as much as she could from all outsiders – were well understood. A visitor would be kept away from the drawing room where she wrote, or, upon entering, would find her in a cap and work-smock as if jotting a shopping list.
>
> *(Honan, 1987: 352)*

Austen persisted, as biographer Park Honan explains, despite concerns that notoriety could undermine not only her ability to write as she wished, but potentially also the social status of her family. Specifically to be thought to have to write to make money would undermine the public sense of her family's prosperity.

> She would write 'when sitting with her family', and when alone she had a special protection. She 'wrote upon small sheets of paper, which could easily be put away, or covered with a piece of blotting paper. There was, between the front door and the offices, a swing door which creaked when it was opened', her nephew recorded later, 'but she objected to having this little inconvenience remedied, because it gave her notice when anyone was coming.' If the door was vital, it was the vigilance of the older women that left her secure so that her imagination and recollections were free to interact.
>
> *(Honan, 1987: 352)*

Risk. Briefly here, the notion that the entire enterprise of creative writing relies on an ability to use basic tools of communication in not so basic ways – in instrumental ways, we could say – and regularly to do so, so that someone other than yourself will respond to the results, and perhaps find them appealing. That the time spent and energy expended on translating what is largely a personal enterprise into what you believe to be a valid depiction of a thought, observation or feeling, or all of these – this a definition of risk. Even if the only audience for your work is yourself, this is not a mere listing of things seen or done, or even a statement of facts determined by experience or research. This is conjecture and distinctive exploration – and in that fact alone, there too is risk.

The characteristics of ADVENTURE in creative writing look like this:

Setting off. An adventure involves something started in order for something to ultimately be done. People have been known to joke about 'armchair adventurers' (those who perhaps play games or watch films *about* adventures, but never actually go on an adventure). Over time, a lot of discussions about creative writing have mentioned the importance of 'confronting the blank page'. More likely today 'confronting a blank screen', beginning to physically write is a kind of initiation but not necessarily where your ideas or inventive thoughts began – they may have formed some time before and will likely form further as you write.

Intimidation by blankness recalls philosophic investigations by those such as Aristotle (384–322 BC) and John Locke (1632–1704), who sought to consider the 'tabula rasa' (blank slate) of the individual minds with which we each are born. The intimidation we feel when faced with filling writerly blankness by application of our own abilities, interpretation of our own experiences, and responses to our own feelings joins the logistical, creative, and intellectual challenges of progressing a project.

Of course, not all creative writers are intimidated by the blank page. Some are stimulated, or positively challenged by it. Canadian novelist and poet Margaret Atwood, referring to a scene in George Orwell's novel *Nineteen*

Eighty-Four (1949), considers that 'for a writer there is something compelling about the blank page' (Atwood, 2014). Joyce Carol Oates, who began writing when she was 14 years old, and who has published to date upward of 150 book-length works, says she never faces a blank page because she 'does her thinking apart from writing'. She adds: 'our brains are filled with so much information we project onto it [the page]' (Oates, 2014). Jonathan Franzen, author of the US National Book Award winning novel *The Corrections* (2001), suggests that 'the blank page in the mind has to be filled before you have the courage to face the blank page' (Franzen, 2016). While Japanese writer and winner of the Gunzo Prize for New Writers and the Noma Literary New Face Prize, Sarayata Murata, says 'I really like a blank page' and explains: 'when I'm writing and sit in front of a blank page – I start by drawing the protagonist of the novel' (Murata, 2022). There is clearly little evidence of these writers being intimidated by a blank page.

Progressing. To adventure is to make your way, most often forward, toward something, whatever that something might be. It is not overstating to say all aspects of how, what, when, and why are second to you simply creating movement. The literal moving hand holding a quill or a pencil, the typing fingers as your eyes follow the words appearing on a screen, this physical action is also representative of movement in the abstract, the intuitive, the work of your mind. Your progress can be defined by number of words completed (many creative writers have recorded this daily – and the frequency of this is worthy of further investigation), or by completion of definable structure elements (a stanza, a chapter, a scene), or by addressing an element or elements of theme or plot or aesthetic condition (for example, if a poet has a pattern of sounds in mind). Ernest Hemingway's grandson, Sean Hemingway, recalls his grandfather's writing of *For Whom the Bell Tolls* (1940) this way:

> His regimen was to begin writing at eight-thirty in the morning and continue to until two or three in the afternoon, the same practice he had established with *A Farewell to Arms*. He frequently recorded the number of words he wrote each day which ranged from three hundred to over a thousand.
>
> *(Hemingway, 2019: xv)*

Adventures take place somewhere, but the well-worn adage, often attributed to American philosopher Ralph Waldo Emerson, that 'it's not the destination it's the journey' is a worthwhile appraisal in creative writing because while the final destination (say, a completed work of creative writing) is useful incentive it is the experiences along the way that maintain our momentum.

Exploration. An adventure embraces an expectation of discovery through exploration. As creative writers, we go out while writing (most often metaphorically speaking) in the interests of learning more – about our subjects and themes and, indeed, about creative writing itself. We humans are not the only living things that explore. The practice of exploration informs how other creatures determine both the potential in the world around them and the dangers in it too. Such exploring can include a 'feedback loop', such as in the case of bees heading out from a hive or deer creating trails that stretch between locations of the most desirable feed. Humans see exploration in this way also – with many of our adventures influenced by necessity. We might have domesticated the search for food into a trip to the grocery store, but we still enter the store in search of bargains and new things to consider buying – and storeowners know this very well, as the placement of products and advertising makes abundantly clear.

Exploration is systematic, which differentiates it from simple seeking or casual observation. Exploration is an investigation, in which we critically consider what we observe or we feel. It is therefore a core component of creative writing – perhaps even the reason some of us do it – because it is through creative writing that we creative writers delve into the subjects and themes that inspire us in the first place, that attract and hold our attention, and that make us want to communicate our responses to them. This is not exactly the kind of exploration we see in the sciences, or exactly the kind we see when musicians are investigating new modes of playing an instrument, or exactly the kind that detectives undertake when they seek out clues to evidence that builds a case – and yet, it has elements of these activities, and more.

Creative writing is individual exploration fueled by curiosity (which is a particular kind of learning where we desire to know something, and we desire it enough that we adopt and develop means of investigating it). Writing creatively does not mean that we forgo climbing mountains or traveling to distant cities or diving deep beneath the ocean. It can mean that in creative writing we have found a way of exploring and of satisfying something of our curiosity. The commonly heard belief that we write to 'find out what we think and feel' is the informal way many writers have expressed this exploratory curiosity that powers their writing and, for many of us, keeps us writing over not just one project but again and again, through many projects.

Chance, luck, and fortuitousness. Finally, adventure comes with some expectation of good and bad fortune. Chance and accident are part of that. It is in part why we admire adventurers, for their willingness to confront chance and risk bad fortune. It is more so why we admire *successful* adventurers, because they have (on occasion) beaten physical odds – open oceans, craggy cliffs, the impossible depths of outer space. Or they have solved a puzzle in a field of human endeavor. They have overcome the fear and the likelihood of misfortune. They've beaten mysterious Fate (as it's sometimes called), the machinations of a universe we don't entirely comprehend.

Chance, luck, and fortuitousness favor the successful creative writer. We admire them for it, the writing adventurer who has ignored the perils, or confronted them and in doing so they have reached their destination. Perhaps we think: if we could only be like that, not only would we succeed as creative writers *what else* might be possible?

Making Decisions

Well-known leader in the field of judgment and decision-making psychology, Janet Sniezek, once said:

> Much of what people do, with the exceptions of reflexive and habitual behavior, results from the cognitive processes of deciding. Even a minor decision, such as whether to drive a car, take the bus, or walk to work, involves the coordination of many complex processes.
>
> *(Sniezek, 2015)*

It is therefore inevitable that creative writing involves individual decision-making. We are certainly faced with questions brought about by technical writing challenges, the skills-based questions that can diminish with increased experience, or so we would hope, or that relate to the relationship between subjects and themes and the modes of expression we chose for them. We find ourselves making decisions on structure, voice, and more, where we confirm the applicability of previous approaches or step out of our comfort zone, guided by a desire or necessity to do that. The interaction of content and form in creative writing is made more varied and more open by the combination of intellect and imagination that it involves. Because of this, and because the decisions we are required to make draw on both emotion and on critical understanding (that is on our impressions as well as our analytical abilities) we are challenged in fascinating ways.

Some straightforward examples: we might be certain we can write a lucid account of a historical event based on available evidence, or an acceptable description of something we have recently seen out in the world, or that we can create a speculative statement of what might happen if a particular course of action is taken. However, are we as sure we can do any of these things with an aesthetic intention? Can we employ an exploratory point of view or exploratory points of view? Can we do this with the pleasure of the reader in mind? Can we employ written language in a way that goes beyond the ordinary? Creative writers do these things all the time. One reason for what is conventionally called 'writer's block' (where a writer is unable to move forward on a piece of writing), and why this is most often associated with stalled creative writing, is that complexity of the work at hand does involve decision-making on multiple levels, not all of them defined by logic or reasoning.

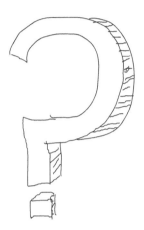

Our writing challenges are informed by our approach to both the venture and the adventure of what we are undertaking, which goes beyond technical considerations. Our questions and the answers, on which we make decisions about what to write and how to write, include the degree to which we might defy or challenge convention, whether aesthetically or in terms of what is told, observed, put on display, or examined. We can be more or less conservative in our creative writing, follow genre conventions or ignore them, attempt to create new forms, or contribute to established ones. Whether we consider our individual personality to be daring or presumptuous or not, we could be said to be engaging in a practice that depends on us being both. This is because creativity involves the new, the novel, and the original, and to engage so directly in it is at the very least ambitious. To varying degrees. Our decision on how we navigate boldness, the venturesome side of creative writing, will define what kind of risks our writing involves. A list could include the risks of time spent, challenges to financial stability, artistic and technical risks in the works themselves, from the macro-elements of choosing a form in which to write to the micro-element of deciding on a particular word to use.

Our decision-making will involve resolving to set off on the undertaking of a piece of creative writing, and taking actions that mean we are, in truth, actually doing it. It will involve blank pages, whether these are a source of angst or a source of joy. And it will mean making some kind of progress. Writing, even by its physical appearance (and sound-recorded writing aims to be an analog of this) involves movement forward, the flow of letters, and the course of words. Progress is built into the physical character of writing.

Not everyone writes creatively for the same reasons, or with the same final results in mind; therefore, knowing the reasons we are writing, and what we want to achieve through it and with it, are poignant reflections. While it might be true that many creative writers seek to see their works published, and have this as their primary goal, other writers emphasize the experience or wish to focus on their self-expression or see the actions of writing creatively as therapeutic. Some write to distribute their works to a smaller, personal audience of friends or relatives.

The venture adventure of creative writing will begin with these decisions partly complete, some essential (the decision to set off into a project, for example) and some evolving as you write. To varying degrees, there might be a desire to explore through writing, a tendency not only to create something but also to investigate something, find out, learn, and discover. So often, creative writing is as much about discovery as it is about prior discoveries, about observations already made, thoughts and feelings already in place. Making such new discoveries is one important attraction for many of us creative writers. Finally, our venture adventure in creative writing will not all be predictable. No matter how technically skilled we become, or whether we plan every element, creative writing involves chance, luck, and fortuitousness. Ours is a practice of the imagination, and the imagination draws on sensations and memories, parts of our brains that are not limited by what we know for sure, have experienced, or can see in the world around us.

References

Atwood, Margaret, https://channel.louisiana.dk/video/margaret-atwood-facing-blank-page, 2014 (Last Accessed, January 7, 2024).

Brodsky, Joseph, 'Aesthetics and Language', in *Nobel Prize Lectures: From the Literature Laureates, 1986–2006*, New York: New Press, 2007, presented by the Nobel Foundation, pp. 255–267.

Franzen, Jonathan, *The Corrections*, New York: Farrar, Straus and Giroux, 2001.

Franzen, Jonathan, Louisiana Channel, https://channel.louisiana.dk/video/jonathan-franzen-facing-blank-page, 2016 (Last Accessed, January 5, 2024).

Grogan, Daniel, *Origins of a Journey: History's Greatest Adventures Marked by Ambition, Necessity and Madness*, Kennebunkport: Appleseed, 2020.

Hemingway, Sean, 'Introduction', in Ernest Hemingway *For Whom the Bells Tolls*, New York: Scribner, 2019, pp. xiii–xxiii.

Honan, Park, *Jane Austen: Her Life*, New York: Ballantine, 1987.

Murata, Sayaka, Louisiana Channel, https://channel.louisiana.dk/video/sayaka-murata-on-facing-the-blank-page, 2022 (Last Accessed, January 5, 2024).

Oates, Joyce Carol, Louisiana Channel, https://channel.louisiana.dk/video/joyce-carol-oates-facing-blank-page, 2014 (Last Accessed, January 5, 2024).

Orwell, George, *Nineteen Eighty-Four*, London: Secker and Warburg, 1949.

Sniezek, Janet A., 'Decision Making', in *Adolescent Health and Wellness*, Paul Moglia (ed), Ipswich: Grey House, 2015, pp. 908–911.

3

METAPHORICALLY SPEAKING

Our Magnetic Journey

> Every mind has a new compass, a new direction of its own, differencing its genius and aim from every other mind. (Emerson, 1903: 306)

In the practice of creative writing, we can refer to a number of conceptual metaphors that have grown over time to become conventional, and they widely influence our thinking about creative writing. Metaphors are designed to catch our attention and to inform us. Not always abruptly: they can be gentle and unhurried. They can be social or they can be intimate. A metaphor extends an idea, a thought, a feeling, gives it greater depth, and, using comparison, helps us apply and extend our knowledge. What we are talking about here in *The Creative Writing Compass* is conceptual metaphor – which is a metaphor or metaphors where one thing assists us to understand another. Conceptual metaphors enhance and, in interesting ways, empower our conceptual abilities – that is, the ways we think and the ways we feel. The creative writing compass here is aimed at assisting us to understand our writerly actions and, by furthering our understanding, to equip us to better employ a range of approaches to our creative writing. Like the magnetic compass, our creative writing compass is a concrete reference to what is abstract: our feeling, our thinking, our interpreting of

DOI: 10.4324/9781003174400-3

what is around us, the layering and intersecting of these when we are writing creatively.

More formally, drawing on cognitive linguistics, Zoltan Kovecses points out that:

> metaphor is defined as understanding one conceptual domain in terms of another conceptual domain.
>
> *(Kovecses, 2010: 4)*

Topically, for us, he goes on to say that:

> A conceptual metaphor consists of two conceptual domains, in which one domain is understood in terms of another. A conceptual domain is any coherent organization of experience. Thus, for example, we have coherently organized knowledge about journeys that we rely on in understanding life.
>
> *(Kovecses, 2010: 4)*

Journeys and compasses! Like Emerson's, Kovecses's choice of example reminds us that journey, direction, and navigation metaphors have been used throughout time, and that they draw on our belief that life itself is a kind of journey, from a beginning to an end, from relative ignorance of what is around us to varying degrees of knowledge, from little understanding at birth to greater understanding as we mature.

One of the most well-known books on metaphor, *Metaphors We Live by*, by linguist George Lakoff and philosopher Mark Johnson, begins with a statement about metaphor's role in our lives:

> The concepts that govern our thought are not just matters of the intellect. They also govern our everyday functioning, down to the most mundane details. Our concepts structure what we perceive, how we get around in the world, and how we relate to other people. Our conceptual system thus plays a central role in defining our everyday realities. If we are right in suggesting that our conceptual system is largely metaphorical, then the way we think, what we experience, and what we do every day is very much a matter of metaphor.
>
> *(Lakoff and Johnson, 1980: 3)*

Conceptual metaphors, the authors suggest, include **structural metaphors**, where 'one concept is metaphorically structured in terms of another' (14), **orientational metaphors**, that 'have to do with spatial orientation: up-down, in-out, back-front, on-off, deep-shallow, central-peripheral' (14) and

ontological metaphors, which are 'usually self-evident, direct descriptions of mental phenomena' (28), providing concrete points of reference for what otherwise would be abstract thoughts and feelings. Kovecses explains:

> The two domains that participate in conceptual metaphor have special names. The conceptual domain from which we draw metaphorical expressions to understand another conceptual domain is called *source domain*, while the conceptual domain that is understood this way is the *target domain*. (my italics)
>
> *(Kovecses, 2010: 4)*

Lakoff and Johnson tell us why this is notable:

> many of our experiences and activities are metaphorical in nature and that much of our conceptual system is structured by metaphor. Since we see similarities in terms of the categories of our conceptual system and in terms of the natural experiences we have (both of which may be metaphorical), it follows that many of the similarities we perceive are the result of conventional metaphors that are part of our conceptual system.
>
> *(Lakoff and Johnson, 1980: 147)*

We are immersed in a world in which we create and are informed by conceptual metaphors. Much of what we perceive and understand about the world, about ourselves, about our actions is affected and effected by these and when they are widely used, within society generally or within particular social, cultural, or even professional groups, these become what Lakoff and Johnson refer to as 'conventional'.

Creative Writing Concepts

Conceptual metaphors in creative writing that have risen to the point of being conventional and influential include:

Craft. Knowing creative writing involves an abstract idea of the imagination and versions of the practical act of inscribing words 'on paper' (that is, writing), the word and concept of 'crafting' has been used to both suggest its concrete meaning of 'making' with 'skill' and its more abstract condition of constructing by hand, laboring, carving out and honing. The conventional condition of this metaphor is such in creative writing that the term 'craft' is common in creative writing teaching and learning. It is the subject of numerous books, and in many countries informs much of the thinking about how creative writing happens. We can ponder this metaphor in the titles of such

American works as *The Emotional Craft of Fiction: How to Write the Story Beneath the Surface* (2016) by Donald Maas, or the well-known *The Art of Fiction: Notes on Craft for Young Writers* (1984), by John Gardner. Emotion and youth meet in Maas and Gardner's craft. The advice given in these books is couched in terms of the knowledge and labor entailed, and we find in both of them a suggestion of a set of technical requirements – the kinds of things a structured and systematic communication like writing involves – and of the psychological and cultural context of the human imagination that creativity entails.

Tellingly, craft can also refer to a trade or occupation that involves skill and dexterity. In that, we sense the conceptual metaphor expands to encompass the ways in which we have long grounded creative writing in equally educational and experiential ways. We have also suggested, in making crafting a conventional metaphor, that while it might be possible to write creatively by accident, or to write our best work in moments rather than days or months or years, it is more likely that it will take time, and that any sudden emergence of writerly brilliance is therefore the result of developed expertise and experience (much as it is in any human profession). Craft, in this way, is a metaphor related to the widely held value of creative writing (including valuing its artistry and our thoughts on its economic value). It also relates to the suggestion that the knowledge and expertise possessed by creative writers is unique, and to the degree of inventiveness and ingenuity creative writing should involve. None of this might be one-hundred-percent true – but its influence on us as metaphor is profound.

Drafting. Here the conventional suggestion is that creative writing is always preliminary. Drafts, drafting, first draft, final draft – these all point toward a technical process in which we iterate, enhance, and develop our writing. Even a final draft is metaphorically imbued with both iteration and enhancement.

A final draft's relationship with the notion of finished creative writing is complex because drafting underpins this and that entails a sequential sense of how writing works. Finished or complete, suggests no more drafting can occur, and the conventional metaphor concerned with creative writing suggests many creative writers are never entirely finished drafting – even if they have stopped writing. Colloquially, we at times hear statements along the lines of 'the first draft ended up being my final draft'. These statements are delivered as exceptions to a rule, anomalies.

Drafting is a powerful conventional metaphor in creative writing because, in addition to its reference to a process, it expands our perception into thoughts on what is preliminary and what is complete, along with ideas about movement (one draft to another) and about building upon (drafting always suggests a succession of actions and results that aim to improve a piece of writing). There is also a weight to this metaphor – not only because draft has other definitions, including that concerned with weights and measures (though draft does indeed have a meaning related to loads and volume) but because this metaphor carries the weight of expectation. Drafting always suggests positive change, movement toward the better – which is why we are disappointed when a later draft does not seem better than an earlier one.

Workshopping. A term widely used in creative writing teaching. The conceptual metaphor here is also associated with craft, and with drafting; but, here the convention is pointing specifically to a writerly work ethic. Seemingly, there is an element of industrialism too, related to the awareness of a workshop as a place where light industry happens (the automobile workshop or the carpenter's workshop). However, the origins of the metaphor long preceded the industrial revolution and are bound up with the idea of a shop as a place on a pre-industrial farm where things were serviced or repaired, and a shop as a place where things are sold. Both references originated in the 15th century. In either case, there is a vocational sense – and we see that as a primary part of the creative writing metaphor too. We workshop creative writing in a creative writing class because creative writing involves effort and skill and because being a creative writer is presented as a vocation. The contrast in this conceptual metaphor is with the idea that creative writing might happen with minimal effort and that everyone can be a creative writer. Clearly workshopping suggests only those who work at it can be creative writers, and that those who consider it as a calling or a trade are the norm.

Less conventional conceptual metaphors that can be found in the practice of creative writing include such random examples as:

- **The building blocks of a novel** – a structural metaphor, where 'one concept is metaphorically structured in terms of another'.
- **A shallow, static or flat character in a short story** – this is an example of an orientational metaphor, which 'have to do with spatial orientation: up-down, in-out, back-front, on-off, deep-shallow, central-peripheral'.
- **The beat of a poem** – an ontological metaphor, involving 'self-evident, direct descriptions of mental phenomena'.

In each case, these metaphors are seeking to move between the source domain ('building block', 'shallow, static, flat', 'beat') and the target domain (the practice of creative writing) to provide us with more information and enhance our understanding. These are not only ways of thinking about what we do or experience when we encounter a finished work of creative writing; importantly, they are ways of thinking when we are engaged in the writing itself. They help us think on the actions we are taking when we are writing.

A Compass

The compass is the practical conceptual metaphor here in this book, the source domain, because it equally combines elements of orientation, interpretation, and movement. An ancient navigational device, a compass situates you in a place and in a time. That is because where you are and when you are constitute elements of navigation. A compass is also relational. It tells you your location relative to somewhere else.

In the well-known magnetic compass, generally thought to have been invented in China during the Han dynasty, the comparative location is magnetic north at the present time. Because the Earth's magnetic poles relate to the movements occurring between the solid inner and molten outer cores of our planet, the magnetic poles shift. Based on the internal movements, currents and convections are happening constantly and, it has long been theorized (Bullard, 1949), creating a dynamo. This dynamo generates the Earth's magnetic field. That magnetic field begins in the inner core of the Earth but extends out into space. It is therefore both of the Earth and related to the expanse beyond it as well. To navigate, you consult the compass, the needle turns until it points you to the Earth's north magnetic pole, and you are then able to plot a course.

With this in mind, a compass metaphor commonly refers to setting a goal, navigating geography to reach that goal and traversing varieties of terrain along the way. Because a compass is useful when you're required to make choices, it also is relevant to moments of creative and analytical thought. If we playfully consider the compass metaphor further we can examine such things as what we mean by our true north – in this case an ideal state that you seek to reach in your creative writing, or in a particular creative writing project. This will likely be a place (or goal) that is authentic to you, encapsulating your writerly purpose. In other words, it would be the figurative right direction for you. We find our bearings by reading (on our compass) where we are in relation to where we seek to go.

The metaphorical *creative writing compass* works in these ways, guiding the creative writer toward a primary destination and providing a practical instrument relating to the dynamo of thinking and imagining, informed by changes that occur while writing, internally in thoughts and in the imagination and externally, in the world beyond you. Adopting the metaphor, your writerly compass, therefore, is not merely a contrivance or a gimmick, it is conceptual, and in this sense is related to our long human tradition of using conceptual metaphors. You can use this metaphor in a number of ways, such as these:

To imagine the shape of a piece of creative writing. What does the 'terrain' look like?

To consider the direction a work is heading, as we are drafting it.

To determine the beginning and end of a work – because a compass is used from your starting point, with an end point in mind.

To focus on what is most in sight and what is less in sight (the primary concerns of a piece of writing, the secondary concerns, the tertiary. . . and so on)

To relate writing actions taken to expected destinations.

A primary challenge in creative writing is to make technical choices that enhance our compositional decisions (that is, our choice of techniques informing our manner of writing). In that sense, we can find ourselves discovering a work we are making as much as we are composing it. But we are also looking for ways to bring imaginative decision-making together with the structural conditions of writing. The compass metaphor assists with this – because every writing action might or might not take us toward the destination we have been imagining. Creative writing is not predetermined. Because the imagination is combinatory and connective, it draws on memories and current observations and feelings, weaves these together, layers them, and creates. Even the most formulaic of creative writing genre (romantic comedy or westerns perhaps) are subject to the influence of our human imaginations. So, while it is possible to make decisions on how to write something, it is not entirely possible (or likely beneficial) to limit options, or to suggest we can program ourselves to stick only to one route, rely only on some environmental influences, or apply only some skills. What we need are our individual compasses to assist with our direction-finding and confirm where it is that we might ultimately arrive.

Core Values

In device terms and in short, a compass is an instrument based on using a magnetized spinning needle pointing to magnetic north (which differs from true north, in that true north is a fixed point on the Earth, while magnetic north alters over time as changes occur in the Earth's magnetic core). The angle between magnetic north and true north is known as magnetic declination, and we need to know the declination value in order to determine the location of true north based on our compass needle direction.

We could consider this, figuratively, when we're writing creatively – and do that by imagining not a fixed north (that is, a fixed result of our creative writing) but, rather, a creative result that emerges along the way, one that might change and evolve as you write, and ultimately be different to the result you had envisaged. Available evidence in numerous writers' diaries and memoirs suggests very few creative writing projects end up identical to how their writers originally perceived them. The figurative 'magnetism' reference is therefore a useful way of bearing in mind that creative writing is a fluid, often shifting activity in which our expectations, while important, need to include our acknowledgment of the vibrant interplay of imagination and intellect.

You cannot write creatively by being unimaginative. However, we can also consider figuratively here that declination depends upon how the magnetic pole and true north align relative to a given point on Earth. A general compass condition is therefore always relative, and it is about alignment. So, also, is your specific creative writing compass – it is *relative in terms of the direction you are heading* (toward what creative result or results?), aligned according to your desires, aims, intentions and influences.

Relative in terms of the direction you are heading, indeed. Brian Clegg, in his book *Ten Patterns that Explain the Universe* (2021), explains the origins of Albert Einstein's celebrated ideas on relativity:

> Einstein was inspired to think about the relationship between space and time that lies at the heart of special relativity by some of the patents that were part of his day job. At the time, the advent of the railways meant that keeping the same time in different locations had become important. In the past, each town had kept its own time, which could vary considerably from location to location. It wasn't possible to run a railway on

such a temporally fragmented basis. As a result, Einstein had to check a number of patents for methods of synchronizing electronic clocks. One of the earliest thoughts he had on special relativity was about the 'relativity of simultaneity' – what is meant for two events, occurring at remote locations, to genuinely happen at the same time.

(Clegg, 2021: 34–35)

Einstein's thoughts, there in the Patent Office in the Swiss capital, Bern, were not about the devices he was examining. Rather, they were focused on his realization that time and space needed to be considered in a certain way to explain the phenomenon that the devices were trying to address. The undertaking and understanding of creative writing is not dissimilar.

If creative writing were just a matter of working out how to compose words in a journey from a start to finish, in a way that made some kind of sense, then our role would simply be to put words in a line, and repeat that action, for however long, until we had a poem or a story. But the metaphoric device we need, and the method, is more complex (and, many of us would argue, far more interesting.).

As core values in creative writing, we are endeavoring to encapsulate thoughts, feelings, observations, information, and responses, and to communicate in a way that travels from one human experience to another. To make *that* work we need an integrated and connected sense of the activity we are undertaking – one that draws on our personal desires and interest. In other words, a sense of things that is relative.

The Importance of Relativity

Albert Einstein's thoughts on the relativity are a brilliant reference point for us as creative writers. The key to them is that *simultaneity is not absolute*. The clue is the observer's observational frame of reference – your frame of reference, in this case, as a creative writer. That frame is relative.

We don't have to become Einsteinians to do some creative writing, or to understand it. However, Einstein's ideas bear some useful fruit for those of us writing creatively.

Imagine you're endeavoring to write a novel that you know has themes and subjects, contains characters and a plot, consists of descriptions and exposition and dialogue, has a narrator or narrators, adopts various points of view and tones, and ultimately is aiming to communicate something to someone. We're dealing in all this with multiple dimensions of engagement and understanding – some of it separated by distance and time (the composing of the novel is not often the same time as the reading of the novel by someone else) and some of it separated by the things we want to achieve and the way in which the reader will perceive what we are saying and construct any meaning from it.

In the most general of senses, as writers we're in an Einsteinian situation: we're trying to understand separation in order to traverse it; that is, to travel from feelings and thoughts to the things we put on a page, to create something that emerges from the self but make it appealing as a communication to others and to situate our observational frame of reference not only in relation to other frames of reference (those of an audience or readers) but also in relation to how the work we're creating might encapsulate things that are encapsulated in other ways in other forms of communication or art. For example, some of the greatest explorations of human compassion or cruelty, of ambition or persistence, of empathy or indifference are found in works of creative writing. But we also see these aspects of human life investigated in other fields (and other writing) – in psychology, sociology, in history, in criminology, in other art forms such as painting. As creative writers, our engagement, our frame of reference, is distinctive to the mode of art and communication we are choosing.

A compass that can assist on a creative writing project is therefore **multidimensional** – a metaphoric device that has (a) an operational aspect and (b) a depth of operation. Meaning, that your compass is not endeavoring to detect just one, clearly observable thing and help us orientate ourselves in relation to a singular 'north pole' – rather, what we're endeavoring to achieve is detecting multiple aspects, and in doing so keeping us on track. Like this:

Physical directions. A creative writing project conceivably begins at the first inscription, the first mark on the page, and finishes at the last one. We can acknowledge a range of theoretical positions that highlight the role of readers in determining how a piece of writing is interpreted, the cultural positioning, the background, and the likely ways a work of creative writing will be generally received. But the fact is writing, at its most obvious, is a set of physical marks. These marks are placed in a direction, which is dependent on the language we're using, and in relation to the medium we're marking up, and most often a creative writer has a basic idea of starting to mark up and of finishing marking up. How we navigate this is interesting – because the idea that creative writers always start at the opening of a work and finish at the closing of it is not always accurate. Some writers begin with something that interests them – which might end up, physically, in the center of the finished work, or at the end. Some writers consciously begin at the end. Some jump from one set of words to another set, entirely because their thoughts jumped around – and then perhaps later join those things they initially etched. The aspects of navigation here – the things a compass assists us to interpret – are at one level very simple: that is, what appears to us, the marks we make. We can track these. On another level, this is complex because we are navigating appearances, how words look on the page, what we know traditionally to be the appearance of certain creative writing forms (a poem, a story, a script), and how the physical marks we make represent meanings. Recognizing this is the beginning of having a compass to interpret these things. Being both aware of the simple physicality of writing ('making marks' to represent and exchange words is remarkably efficient) and the complexity of the choices we have – in word selection, grammar, punctuation; how things look on a page and how each block (paragraph, page, stanza) relates to what is around it.

Transcendental. Whether we believe creativity is associated with inspiration or with imitation (over time, both these have been considered creative), whether it is about complete freedom or the adherence to certain rules or laws of artistic expression, whether associated with certain people (poets, for example) and not with others, or whether not associated with people primarily but rather something from the realm of a god, creativity (which emerged as a term only in the 17th century) has been correlated with transcending the ordinary and engaging with the spiritual. Sometimes this has been allied to creating something from nothing – and further identified with the supernatural and magical. Sometimes this has been married to shaping and combining, to the role of the creative writer (say) in raising up some things and in diminishing others. By attempting to follow this, to give ourselves a sense of the direction we're going, or the one we feel we need to go, we're not presenting the transcendental as more ordinary. Rather, we're allowing ourselves the counsel of the metaphysical – the intangible – and we're keeping in mind that every creative writing project has in some way been borne out of the sacred (what we value in human creativity, not necessarily in a religious sense but in the sense of being regarded with respect).

Conceptual. We have a sense of what we want to achieve in creative writing and not everything is a material thing. In each creative writing project, nascent or sketchy, we have a concept of the project and of why we are doing it. The reasons might shift around, we might be more or less sure during the project, more or less confident, but we seek out and endeavor to maintain something we have conceived. Something stimulated by internal or external forces but conceived in our minds. This internal conceptualizing, regardless of the original stimulus for it, means that we are both owners of and responsible for how we develop, maintain, and pursue our project. Our compass, in other words, is our own.

Relational. Any project we pursue in creative writing naturally generates comparative information because it exists in the world in which other things are happening. This includes information about how it is related to those other things – between that project and what we might have otherwise chosen to write; between what we are writing and what has already been written (on the subject or theme, in other creative writing forms, perhaps at different points throughout time). These things as well as eliciting a response focused on what we otherwise might be doing, other ways we might be spending our time and effort. Howard Gardner, in his book *Creating Minds*, speaks about extreme versions of this:

> the creators were so caught up in their pursuit of their work mission that they sacrificed all, especially the possibility of a rounded personal existence.
>
> *(Gardner, 1983: 44)*

Perhaps we do not always 'sacrifice all', as Gardner puts it, but we do prioritize. It is not simply that we navigate personal choice to write creatively – which we very often do – it is also the focus on a particular project, which produces a pattern of interactions with that which is around us with people, places, other aspects of life. We can follow this and keep it in mind. We can think relationally to give us a sense of our intention and reasoning in doing a particular project or projects, and we can remind ourselves of other works and other writers who have pursued similar projects (or entirely different ones too) and use these things as reference points for what, why, and how we are going about our work.

An emotional compass. Developing an emotional compass sounds compelling but somewhat forced. After all, there are no grounds on which to suggest that we creative writers are any more (or less) able to detect, assess, and master our emotions than anyone else. And yet, one of the reasons people connect with the work of creative writers is almost certainly the exchange of emotional contexts, the consideration of feelings, and the suggestion (however slight) that many types of creatively written works provide insights into our human condition and assist us in better understanding human emotions. It is one of the reasons we encourage children to read literature – not simply to develop their literacy skills but also to learn to better comprehend human mental states, in this way in order to encourage positive emotions through understanding. A creative writer's emotional compass might not be a direction finder for their own emotional states – but it can be a finder for what emotional contexts they're seeking to portray in their work, and why, and how they're portraying them. That kind of compass, especially when we know works of creative writing build bridges between one human and another, provides information on focal points, on where scenes rather than summary might occur, on choice of words and tone, and on voice. This kind of tool is engaging us in how we are communicating consequently in frames of reference (subject, content, action) and in frames of mind.

Formal (such as relates to genre). Genres provide their own guidance because they have their own sense of direction and points of interest. The definition of genre effectively suggests this by referring to style and to categorization. The suggestion about popular genre is that these directions and points are more predetermined, whereas in work considered more literary the entirety of the journey is speculative and open to interpretation. This rule of thumb has some value – not least because readers and audiences for a particular genre (the romance, the fantasy novel, the first-person shooter game, the movie thriller) do come to the genre with relatively established expectations, and therefore their pleasure can be related to a writer meeting those expectations. But this rule of thumb also comes with provisos – such as, that form and its function can become banal, and therefore uninteresting, if not individualized; such as, that genre is defined also by culture and by history, making its compass directions contextual as well as textual.

Systematic (as relates to language). The language compass, because language comes with conventions; that is, with understood and shared meanings. Without maintaining these, and empowering them, we lose connection between writer and audience and potentially the unstated agreement that there is a shared venture in creative writing. In more acute cases of separation, communication becomes all but impossible, because language use by a writer becomes so individualized as to undermine the system of shared meaning. There are some basic considerations here such as those related to idiom and the vernacular. Other considerations relate to how much convention defines meaning – given that creative writing has the opportunity to stretch and expand language use, to delve into the less well-known aspects of a language, where nuances of interpretation can be found (in uncommon words or in colloquialisms representing marginalized groups). It therefore offers creative writers, and the readers and audiences for the works of creative writers, the joy of discovering more about an otherwise familiar language (such as in the linguistic play in the work of American poet E.E. Cummings, for example – in such works in *ViVa*, published in 1931). This might also occur at the level of national or cultural heritage or at the level of the specialized languages of places or occupations (for instance, in the annual gatherings in the USA of 'fisher poets' and of 'cowboy poets').

Compositional. A directional sense of writerly action. One of the challenges beginning creative writers face is in defining and gaining confidence in the series of actions their creative writing most often entails. Many books – and this could be one of them – and many courses in creative writing seek to provide models of how to look at creative writing in terms of drafting, revising, and editing in order to build confidence in what is often described as 'the writing process'. While such books and courses might not make the suggestion this can be reduced to a single model, there is sometimes a practical outcome that builds those actions into a series, a beginning, middle, and end for 'the writing process'- even though how any series of actions is understood is itself best considered as personalized. The issue here lies in examining how your own writing comes about. While drawing on models from other writers, from other creative practices, indeed from any other human activity that particular examination begins in the recognition that there is no fixed or immutable 'series' of compositional actions that must take place. Rather, there is a fluidity.

Your creative writing compass is more than a device. It is, more than a thing, more than a plan, more than a method, more than something you pick up and apply – and similarly, so is the traditional compass used by seafarers and adventurers. And that is why this book uses the compass as its overarching metaphor. Compasses have always required and encouraged human interpretation. They have never systematized journeys; rather, they have supported them. We also think and act this way when writing creatively because although we can talk about literary devices or methods of composing, our activities as writers entail intersecting emotions, beliefs and analyses. They involve structuring and formalizing as is required for intelligible written communication. This is combined with an openness that comes from dealing in the new and the original; with the inventive, the playful, the ingenious, the intuitive and the transcendent. All of which are fundamental characteristics of creativity.

References

Bullard, Edward Crisp, 'The Magnetic Field within the Earth', *Proceedings of the Royal Society of London. Series A, Mathematical and Physical Sciences*, 197, no. 1051, July 7, 1949, pp. 433–453.

Clegg, Brian, *Ten Patterns That Explain the Universe*, Boston: MIT Press, 2021.

Cummings, Edward Estlin, *ViVa*, New York: Liverright, 1997 (first published 1931).

Emerson, Ralph Waldo, *The Complete Works of Ralph Waldo Emerson*, Cambridge, MA: Riverside Press, 1903.

Gardner, John, *The Art of Fiction: Notes on Craft for Young Writers*, New York: Alfred A. Knopf, 1984.

Kovecses, Zoltan, *Metaphor: A Practical Introduction*, 2nd ed., Oxford: Oxford University Press, 2010.

Lakoff, George and Mark Johnson, *Metaphors We Live By*, Chicago: University of Chicago Press, 1980.

Maass, Donald, *The Emotional Craft of Fiction: How to Write the Story Beneath the Surface*, New York: Writer's Digest Books, 2016.

Schmandt-Besserat, Denise, 'Writing, Evolution of', in *International Encyclopedia of the Social & Behavioral Sciences*, 2nd ed., James D. Wright (ed), Oxford: Elsevier, 2015, pp. 761–766.

4

WRITING WITH RISK

The Writing Art

Writing is . . .

> humankind's principal technology for collecting, manipulating, storing, retrieving, communicating and disseminating information. Writing may have been invented independently three times in different parts of the world: in the Near East, China and Mesoamerica.
>
> *(Schmandt-Besserat, 2015: 763)*

Creative writing is clearly all that – the 'collecting, manipulating, storing, retrieving, communicating and disseminating'. As creative writers we collect impressions and knowledge (often personal knowledge) and material that stimulates our imaginations; we certainly offer (most often) individual interpretations of what we observe, discover, or feel, and this could be considered a type of 'manipulation'; we form and store ideas and often draw on memories, immediate and long-established; we seek out directly and indirectly, retrieving from the world around us the things we need for our work; and we communicate and disseminate all in a variety of forms – which are indeed culture-specific, informed by our histories and our societies and experiences.

Most importantly, creative writing is a form of art. This quality, above all else, defines its difference to other forms of writing. Though it might be argued other forms of writing involve creativity, the creativity in other forms of writing is not as heightened as it is in creative writing. The end results of us writing creatively, the works we create, are endowed with aesthetic intention; and these works come about because we have aesthetic results in mind as we write.

DOI: 10.4324/9781003174400-4

We write creatively with sensory as well as communicative values, our emotions, sensibilities, and sentiments informing our choices along perceived facts and frequently indeterminate and nonspecialist knowledge. We draw on our contemporary world to consider style and form, as well as our content, reviewing current tastes, either to follow them or to challenge them. An awareness of the writing arts market is common for creative writers, and a sense of writing for or outside of that market is often present as we work, even if our sharing of our works of creative writing might be entirely non-commercial, and the undertaking nothing to do with the mercantile value. The intrinsic personal and communal value of creative writing relates to its ingenuity, and originality, and newness, and imaginativeness as well as to its communicative strengths.

Generally, the origins of writing are connected to orality, to storytelling, and in this storytelling not only were words involved but our bodies as well. Writing began as an identifiable kind of physical activity where words were part of a shared physiological and psychological experience. As Sylvia Pinheiro and her colleagues explain:

> Before the invention of writing, the ability to narrate real or fictional events was nearly exclusively mediated by oral storytelling, aided by gestural and postural communication. Short-range recurrence was likely favored because it facilitates rhyme and rhythm, as well as the memorization of short strings of words.
>
> *(Pinheiro et al., 2020: 8)*

That is, gestural and postural communication bound up most often in the pursuit of clarity and of the particular. In other words, in ensuring a specific thing or things (for example, a thought, a request, an emotion) was exchanged with minimal chance of miscommunication. From the time of its invention, we quickly came to revere writing and to see in it the possibilities for creativity. Walter Stephens writes:

> Throughout history, humans have regarded the art of writing with awe and reverence. To imagine humanity without writing was not impossible, but it was in many ways difficult. . . .
>   Throughout five millennia, **the art of writing has always been paradoxical**, as mundane and practical as a pencil, yet miraculous, more stupefying in its way than its end products like *Paradise Lost*, the *Divine Comedy*, the *Iliad*, or, ultimately, the Babylonian epic of *Gilgamesh*. [my emboldening]
>
> *(Stephens, 2023: xi)*

Learning writing most often during our childhoods, those of us in the world's literate cultures (that is, cultures that write and read) reduce the risk of miscommunication, misdirection, and misunderstanding by being encouraged to learn to write in a way that is unambiguous. The timing of this learning is notable, because it is also in childhood that we are discouraged by those who care for us from taking other risks too – physical, certainly, communicative clearly; but also sometimes cultural, intellectual risks, and others. In fact, in whatever culture, and in whatever household, the emphasis on protecting children from risk is generally held sacrosanct.

Risk aversion manifests itself in writing not only in generally favoring clarity but in being explicitly aware of the dangers of taking risks in relation to meaning, in conveying our intentions, or in our complicating communication by using language, linguistic structures, or a system of notation that unsettles or challenges the ways in which our (now largely screen-based) writing might convey through words what once would be often accompanied by our gestures and postures. In many of today's professional fields – say Medicine, Computer Science, Chemistry – writing in the field is only truly comprehensible to those with expertise in the field. Not only is this defining disciplinary knowledge, it is also a method of ensuring that those who have that knowledge can convey it within their professional communities somewhat exclusively. When in some instances – and we might include the law in this – writing allows for higher degrees of interpretation and greater potential for alternative opinions of meaning and intention, considerable attention has been applied to reducing the risk in those written communications by creating roles (attorneys, for example, government officials) whose job it is to reduce the risk of disagreement.

In short, and in so many instances, in writing in today's world we actively avoid risk. This is not so much the case in creative writing, because it is also a form of art.

Communication Paradox

In artistic work, the ideal is not to rationalise and regulate the self and the body. It is rather the opposite, artistic ideal includes immediacy, spontaneity, contemporality, scarification and irrationality. . . .

In today's creative discourse, artistic and economic risk taking tend to be mixed up in a large pot commonly known as creative labour. The new creative worker is flexible, autonomous and independently working in "a dazzling environment of creative autonomy, sensory stimulation and personal fulfilment"

(Kleppe, 2017: 63)

The ideal that Bård Kleppe identifies here in his article in the journal *Poetics* is referring to the work of performing artists, but also relates to us creative writers. The creative arts involve forms of risk, and in creative writing no less so than in the other arts. Of course, creative writers moreover use a form of expression and communication that is used for other purposes – day to day purposes, explanatory purposes, informational purposes, instructional purposes, and so much more. That element of clarity and an aversion to miscommunication, misdirection, and misunderstanding is therefore manifest in our daily lives.

While amusing to imagine a communication to work colleagues written in lyric poetry or a thriller screenplay used to communicate directions for traveling to the grocery store, our general approach is not overtly a creative, artistic use of writing but a pragmatic one – and it is in this fact that Bård Kleppe's observations become a starting point, because it is fundamentally in risk that creative writing differentiates itself from other forms of writing. That is, by being both venture *and* adventure. In an article entitled 'Intellectual Risk Taking: A Moderating Link Between Creative Confidence and Creative Behavior?' Ronald Beghetto, Maciej Karwowski, and Roni Reiter-Palmon say this:

> successfully taking creative action requires taking the risk of making mistakes and even failing. . . This type of a risk is adaptive because the potential benefits outweigh the potential costs. . . Moreover, a general willingness to take such risks can be thought of as a more stable and general self-belief that develops from more dynamic and situational experiences with risk-taking behaviors.
>
> *(Beghetto et al., 2021: 638)*

Even though 'the specific relationship among adaptive risk taking, creative confidence and creative behavior remains unclear' (Beghetto et al., 2021: 638), the existence of risk-taking in creative action (in our case, in creative writing) is clear, and Bård Kleppe's description assists us in comprehending how we might think on this:

Immediacy. A core consideration in creativity. Talking of 'setting off' into some creative writing is for many paradoxical because the ideal of immediacy in creative writing is variable. For some writers, direct access to stimuli, immediate response to what is around them, or actively sought out is common. In this case, the writers' method of working is immersive, observational, even reactive. For other writers, their mode of engagement is more contemplative, evolutionary, seclusive. Here immediacy might not be primarily about proximity but, rather, about the urgency and excitement felt when a thought, or feeling, or idea begins to generate a creative response. Both definitions of immediacy are relevant in creative writing, and neither is superior. You might be the kind of creator whose sense of closeness to a thing or a person, or experience is essential to setting off (and, indeed, to continuing your writing); or, you might be the kind of creator who is profoundly impelled forward by a sense of needing to write, by the excitement of a thought or feeling that has been developing over some time, perhaps at a distance from the stimuli that first triggered it (for example, a moment of bemusement that years later produces a story or play).

Spontaneity suggests a lack of planning, but this too is paradoxical, because certain creative writers spend a long time outlining what they will do before they do it. So, at first, Kleppe's idea seems flawed. However, spontaneity relates also to natural response, to our actions and reactions based on the indeterminant. Because we use our imaginations in a heightened way during creative writing no amount of pre-planning can undermine that kind of spontaneity. It might be that you have laid out the plot and characters of your short story, the sections of it, and the voice and tone of the narrator. But your imagination, interacting with your intellect, will determine the writing itself. Creative writing is not fixed in place by prior determinations – rather, it is fluidly accomplished. This is both its attraction and part of its formidable nature. It is one thing to follow a plan for an article on a well-researched subject; quite another to set out to tell a story, mapped out or not.

Contemporality. That is, of the now, of the same time as we occupy. According to Bård Kleppe, the artist is focused on what is around them: the attitudes, moods, and influences of the moment, the era, the time. Of course, this doesn't refer to how that contemporaneousness appears in our work – it is a reference to influences, for sure, but not to limitations of response. One of the most powerful aspects of creative writing is its melding, juxtaposing, and contrasting of what is occurring around us with what has occurred or might occur – or with an alternative, personal vision of how something or someone might act. This is memory at work, the processing and encoding of the present and the absent – imaginative reconfiguring, where contemporality can mean directly reported or it can mean indirectly influenced and then presented through our individual creative lenses. It is the miraculous nature of this, whereby a creative writer has produced a work that seems both of its time and somehow beyond it, that has had some critics suggest the practice is more based on mystery than on actual knowledge.

Scarification. Kleppe's choice of word here relates to the etching or scratching that those who scarify their bodies undertake. The suggestion is that artists – performing artists in the case of his analysis – create permanent evidence that is physiologically present as well as intellectually present. Art making, then, as symbolic, perhaps decorative, personal, and indeed potentially painful. The question of how you set off into creative writing knowing that it is likely to bring challenges – some that will have you questioning whether you are capable of doing it (even though you might indeed be entirely competent at writing generally) – is only answered by considering how much you desire to express yourself creatively this way. Creative writing etches itself, metaphorically, on the screens on which most of us work, the inscribing that was once on rock or parchment or paper; but it also scarifies by etching on us, on our own sense of self and self-worth.

Irrationality. Writing creatively does not always bear up – in fact, many times it does not bear up – to an assessment of what is logical. For one thing, using words the way we sometimes use them in creative writing defies how they are used most often (thus, the novel, unique, new aspect associated with creativity) and therefore raises questions about the quality and intention and focus of the communication. For another thing, writing creatively is highly personalized so that whereas some forms of writing very clearly target groups with shared interests, even in the most narrowly defined sense of a genre of creative writing the appeal to all people in any group is reliant on individual style, tone and inventive appeal. The variables are considerable, then, so it is irrational to imagine that as a creative form of writing the end results will appeal to a predictable number in any audience. Of course, the more plainly visible are genre characteristics the more likely initial responses will match expectations. However, inventiveness means speculation not assurance. More irrationally still, because reading works of creative writing is a leisure activity for the majority of people the imperative to engage with creative writing is entirely generated by personal circumstance and interest. If communicating with an audience is a reason for writing creatively then it is irrational to imagine that audience as anything other than idiosyncratic and mostly driven by individual or small group choice (for example, based on the influence of family or friends).

From the perspective of time and effort, it is equally irrational to imagine simply increasing time spent and effort applied will proportionally increase the likelihood of making a career as a creative writer. Because of this, few creative writers can work the majority of their time on their creative writing. Fewer still have an income from their creative writing that rises to the level of a living wage. Therefore, the joy must be in the doing of it not in the likelihood of success when the writing is done, which is also dependent on other parties in the creative industries – in publishing, broadcast media, theater, leisure software, film – who substantially control the means of distribution and for whom the finished results, while culturally or personally valued, might not match their own corporate needs.

What Bård Kleppe calls 'a dazzling environment of creative autonomy, sensory stimulation and personal fulfilment' is also a place of passionate irrationality. Author of *The Waste Land* (1922), T.S. Eliot, once wrote: 'only those who will risk going too far can possibly find out how far one can go' (Eliot, 1931: ii). That journey might be one based on illogic – but one you set out upon, nevertheless, with Eliot's words echoing.

Our Individual Risk

> Perhaps the biggest takeaway from our preliminary study is that our find-
> ings suggest that even if people have confidence in their creativity, they
> seem to also need to be willing to take creative risks.
>
> *(Beghetto et al., 2021: 643)*

Creative Writer's Risk could be the title of an entire book diving deep into
what we are doing when we are using writing as an artistic medium – from
the point of view of the paradox as well as the possibility. The paradox,
meaning to know writing is a mode of communication in pursuit of clarity,
using highly exchangeable visible signs, a system of symbols, conventionality,
and *creative* writing is a form of writing in which expressions and impressions and ideas and observations and feelings are often shared because of
originality, newness, and invention (in other words, because of varying degrees of unconventionality; or, at very least, innovation and distinctiveness).
The possibility, meaning the openness and human imaginative potential of an
art form that uses one of the most common of our communication tools, the
written word, and therefore appears at the most basic level to be addressing
any literate person. There are, of course, nuances in this, considerations of
what learning to read and write entail, and cultural biases that impact, and
economic restrictions. There is no doubt that writing is not available to all
people or to all people to the same degree. And yet, in literate cultures (that
is, in cultures where reading and writing are primary modes of communication) the possibility in creative writing, to be used to share experiences, emotions, ideas, ideals, histories, identities . . . That possibility is considerable.

> Creative behavior is risky behavior. Taking creative action therefore re-
> quires a person's willingness to take adaptive risks, which includes viewing
> the potential hazards involved in taking action as being outweighed by the
> potential benefits.
>
> *(Beghetto et al., 2021: 638)*

The risks artists take, that we take as creative writers, are rarely physical
risks. Only occasionally are they financial risks or risks to reputation. Dereg-
ulation and freedom are the avenues of risk we travel, where we let go of the
requirements of other kinds of writing and embrace novelty, and inspiration,
and inventiveness. Emotional stability and our sense of self – a kind of scarification, as Bård Kleppe describes it – can come with creative writing. While
we can gain pleasure from creative writing, it can also cause us pain – the
painful failures we might ensure, especially being literate individuals who
feel familiar with general writing, the anguish of not knowing if our creative
skills will match the technical needs of a project, the discomfort of wondering

if readers or audiences will enjoy our work. We risk these things. Not to mention those more idiosyncratic histories of creative writers whose high-spirited or unorthodox artist lifestyles, focused on and fueled by their writing, challenged their general well-being.

We creative writers therefore take risks, and some, like the author of such novels as *Ragtime* (1975) and *Billy Bathgate* (1989), E.L. Doctorow, declare that no good writing will emerge without doing so:

> I believe nothing of any beauty or truth comes of a piece of writing without the author's thinking he has sinned against something – propriety, custom, faith, privacy, tradition, political orthodoxy, historical fact, literary convention, or indeed, all the prevailing standards together.
>
> *(Doctorow, 2004: 36–37)*

References

Beghetto, Ronald A., Maciej Karwowski and Roni Reiter-Palmon, 'Intellectual Risk Taking: A Moderating Link Between Creative Confidence and Creative Behavior?', *Psychology of Aesthetics, Creativity, and the Arts*, 15, no. 4, 2021, pp. 637–644.

Doctorow, E. L. *Reporting the Universe* (William E. Massey, Sr., Lectures in the History of American Civilization), Boston: Harvard University Press, 2004.

Eliot, T.S., 'The Waste Land', *The Criterion*, 1, no. 1, October 1922, pp. 50–64.

Eliot, T.S., 'Preface', in *Transit of Venus*, Harry Crosby (ed), Paris: Black Sun Press, 1931, pp. viii–ix.

Kleppe, Bård, 'Theatres as Risk Societies: Performing Artists Balancing between Artistic and Economic Risk', *Poetics*, 64, 2017, pp. 53–62.

Pinheiro, Sylvia, Natalia Bezerra Mota, Mariano Sigmanc, Diego Femandez-Slezal, Antonio Guerreiro, Lufs Fernando Tófoli, Guillermo Cecchii, Mauro Copellii and Sidarta Ribeiro, 'The History of Writing Reflects the Effects of Education on Discourse Structure: Implications for Literacy, Orality, Psychosis and the Axial Age', *Trends in Neuroscience and Education*, 21, 2020, p. 100142.

Schmandt-Besserat, Denise, 'Writing, Evolution of', in *International Encyclopedia of the Social & Behavioral Sciences*, 2nd ed., James D. Wright (ed), Amsterdam: Elsevier, 2015, pp. 761–766.

Stephens, Walter, *How Writing Made Us Human, 3000 BCE to Now*, Baltimore: Johns Hopkins University Press, 2023.

5

MAPS AND OTHER GUIDES

Making a Writing Instrument

Even the most basic tools extend our ability to do things. They facilitate, they assist us, and they help us perform a task. Writing is resplendent with tools. This makes sense, because writing is, of course, the act of inscribing words on something somewhere sometime, *with* something (that is, a tool), so that those words remain after you, the writer, have left that place or time, or so that you can have those words sent out into the world without you.

The book, the origins of which we can trace back to clay tablets in the 3rd millennium BCE, and papyrus around 2400 BCE, is itself a form of tool (a mechanism of creating an exchange through writing). The clay tablet, of course, involved clay, and fire to set the clay, the papyrus had to be pressed and dried and glued and cut. Reed brushes held in ivory or wooden palettes were once used to write on papyrus, with natural pigments, iron oxide, and charcoal.

Writing, which appeared in a nascent form around 35,000 BCE, is equally reliant on as it is resplendent upon tools – and creative writing no less so than any other writing. Importantly, though, the physical conditions of writing – which provide a useful reminder of the physicality of the extent of what we do when we write *creatively* – are also imbued with philosophic, aesthetic, textual, cultural, personal, and communal conditions. In this way, the tools we use represent part of an organic contributory activity, in which writing mechanics play a role, though not independent of the contexts in which we use them. We can cite the invention of physical writing tools – such as the first practical typewriter with QWERTY keyboard invented by C. Latham Sholes in Wisconsin in 1873 – but changing ideas and attitudes,

DOI: 10.4324/9781003174400-5

emotional and cerebral responses contribute to the creation of what we can, metaphorically, consider compasses, maps, and guides to our writing. In many ways these are more important than (and enhance) the physical tools we use because it is these that underpin, empower and inform the reasons, meanings, and intentions of our creative writing – culturally and for each of us individually.

'There has been comparatively little examination of the impact on *creative* writing of changes in writing tools' (Harper, 2023: 18–19). And there has been even less so concerning creative writing instruments. The terms 'tool' and 'instrument' are sometimes used interchangeably. So, an instrument is sometimes called a tool – for measurement, for example. But there are differences between tools and instruments. While tools are considered to be mechanical, instruments are more broadly a means of achieving something. Additionally, while a tool is an implement to make something easier to get done, an instrument may be this but involve more mastery, more interpretation. A tool is a device but an instrument more greatly enables our agency – which is why we call apparatus for playing music 'musical instruments' rather than 'musical tools'. Similarly, when we use the colloquial expression 'a blunt instrument', we mean more than 'a blunt tool', often incorporating such inferences as a perceived lack of intelligent behavior, or a brutishness, or an inability to lead, or a bumbling attempt to force something to happen.

With creative writing, when seen from our writer's point of view, we can also actively consider and endeavor to employ our own creative instrument-making techniques, harnessing our responses to the things we observe, imagine, feel, and analyze, making the instruments we employ to assist us in our writing projects, using our judgment of direction and approach, fluidly, so that our progress is not based on a fixed sense of the north we seek; but, rather, is created and re-created in the actions of writing creatively.

In other words, we might use literal writing tools – a computer, a pencil, a phone, a chisel, a stylus – but we can also use creative writing instruments, literally and figuratively: a compass, a map, other guides.

The Bakersfield Expedition

'The Bakersfield Expedition' and Emily Bronte's desk, a 21st-century television sitcom episode and a 19th-century creative writer's desk, are cases in point. Both these exemplify the intersecting but varying aspects seen when considering writing tools and creative writing instruments. Tools can influence us and their use involves skill. Instruments can empower us and their use involves mastery.

In *The Bakersfield Expedition*, a Season Six episode of the American television sitcom, *The Big Bang Theory*, which first aired on American CBS network on January 10, 2013, four of the main characters are on their way to Bakersfield Comic-Con, when they decide to stop to pose in the Californian desert. Wearing their Comic-Con *Star Trek* costumes, they strike their poses in terrain they imagine is that of an alien planet. Of the four characters, only Sheldon does not pose swinging a punch, deflecting a punch, or pointing a ray gun:

HOWARD: So what's our first pose going to be?
RAJ: I say we begin with a classic *Star Trek* fight scene.
LEONARD: I'll set the timer.
HOWARD: Sheldon, how is that a fight pose?
SHELDON: Mr. Data's weapon is his mind. I'm wielding it.
                                           (Cendrowski, 2013)

A weapon or a tool is an implement or device, and the humor in this scene emerges from the incongruity between the expectation of Howard, Raj, and Leonard that Sheldon will join them in also wielding a tool, and Sheldon's announcement that he is, in fact, 'wielding' an instrument (that is: his mind).

Barbara Heritage, Associate Director and Curator of Collections at the Rare Book School at the University of Virginia, equally ventures skillfully into the intersection and the differences between tool and instrument when she considers Emily Brontë's writing desk:

> I attempt a more holistic look into the writing desk, instruments, and supplies used by Brontë, to suggest how the activities of writing, copying, cutting, and canceling are part of larger, interconnected practices that need to be studied in relation to one another. By learning how to identify these writing implements as well as their visual and tactile traces, we can recover new evidence documenting the many stages of Brontë's writing process that have hitherto remained hidden in plain sight within the very materials of her own bookmaking practices. By learning to "read" the writing desk with a bibliographical eye, an alternative form of interpretation emerges: we can attend to the more corporeal elements of the Brontë corpus.
>
> *(Heritage, 2021: 507–508)*

Heritage's 'bibliographical eye', as she calls it, gets this a little wrong, because she is in fact looking at evidence of writerly action. Though she is correct to recognize the significance of the objects on the desk, and to consider these holistically, it is the experiential nature of what the objects represent that is most significant, their role in the actions of creative writing – the objects represent not 'bookmaking' but creative writing practice. We see here on the desk traces of a writer and writing; and, while they might indeed relate to a 'corpus' of literary works, more notably they relate to a life, a specific person, to that person's responses to the world around them, to their desires, hopes, intentions, and beliefs.

Mapping

In conceptual metaphors. . .

> there is a set of systematic correspondences between the source and the target in the sense that constituent conceptual elements of b correspond to constituent elements of a. Technically, these conceptual correspondences are often referred to as **mappings**.
>
> *(Kovecses, 2010: 7)*

Kovecses's reference to mappings as 'correspondences' (9) pertains to similarities and equivalences, and how such congruities and harmonies make up conceptual metaphors.

We often hear of creative writers 'mapping out' their work – and perhaps seen evidence of this in their doodles, notes, sketches, notes pinned to boards and walls in their rooms, as well as in what we might call some of the more time-honored elements of actual maps (lines, shapes, names).

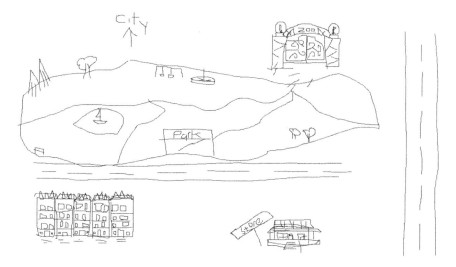

Partial Map for the Brooke Biaz novel, *Releasing the Animals* (Parlor, 2023).

Mapping is a symbolic representation of relationships between things. In the contemporary world, maps can be static or dynamic, fixed on paper or moving on screens. Of course, it would be far-fetched to suggest everything that a creative writer does in this fashion is in some way a map (that is, a symbolic representation of a relationship between one thing and another). And many of the things mentioned – those doodles, for example, those notes – have most often been depictions of what a writer hoped would one day exist when they had finished their particular writing project, not what already existed.

Exemplifying the popular historical account of such writerly things Tara Brady, in an article in Britain's *The Daily Mail* (Brady, 2013), once showed examples of grids and tables and doodles made by writers Henry Miller, J.K. Rowling, Jennifer Eagan and Gay Talese, among others, that in notable ways accomplish the act of mapping. Over time, creative writers themselves, such as the author of *Junkie* (1953) and *Naked Lunch* (1959), William S. Boroughs, have directly mentioned their mapping:

> In my writing I am acting as a map maker, an explorer of psychic areas, a cosmonaut of inner space, and I see no point in exploring areas that have already been thoroughly surveyed.
>
> *(Burroughs, 1977: 13)*

'Surveyed' is a fascinating choice of words by Burroughs. The word has two meanings. The first relates to a general examination, a broad consideration, or description of something. In that sense, you would not go looking to a survey to discover specifics, to find out details, or to enhance conventional shared knowledge. We see that in education where someone is said to offer 'a survey course' – meaning a course that addresses a subject but does so in such a way as to give you a starting point or two for knowing the subject, but not so you can consider yourself an expert. Often, such courses are offered in the early years of a student's higher education and later they are given the opportunity to 'specialize' – meaning to dig deeper and become more informed about a narrow aspect of something they had previously touched upon in a survey.

Burroughs is not using 'surveyed' in this first sense. Instead, he is referencing a second meaning of surveyed. That meaning is surveying as a recording and examination of features, often of land but potentially of anything (we jovially 'survey the mood' in a work meeting, or we 'survey the choices' of breakfast at a budget hotel buffet). To survey is to observe and to assess and to construct our own representation of something – for ourselves and/or for others. We bring to surveying our individual ways of seeing and we bring to surveying our own feelings. As Burroughs suggests, once surveyed we map. Mapping is a natural process of addressing something, closely considering it, and then recording it so that we (ourselves and others) can reference it.

As you read this, you might begin to think how much like this second sense of surveying creative writing happens to be. In the same way, creative writing is not about a broad, general consideration of something; rather, it is an examination in which we consider and record features and we provide this information, these observations, and this record of experience for ourselves and for others. We don't do this without individual interpretation and influence and indeed the impact of our imaginations, applying perspective and allocating varying levels of significance to aspects of what we are considering. All creative writing is like this, and therefore it is no wonder that we creative writers are also drawn to mapping.

Intriguingly, when William Burroughs discusses his own mapping he refers to 'psychic areas' not to physical attributes out in the world. Rita Carter, in her topically named book *Mapping the Mind* (1998), notes 'neuroscientists at the University of California San Diego have located an area in the temporal lobe of the brain that appears to produce intense feeling of spiritual transcendence, combined with a sense of some mystical presence' (Carter, 1998: 13). So our minds are themselves spatial, contain zones, and therefore have routes and relationships between these zones. These zones, and places within them, have specific functions. This is a fascinating discovery in itself, and could represent a metaphoric guide to the way we approach the world and things we find in it.

> What distinguishes the map from the tracing is that it is entirely oriented toward experimentation in contact with the real. The map does not reproduce an unconscious closed in upon itself, it constructs the unconscious.
>
> *(Deleuze and Guattari, 1987: 12)*

Mapping in creative writing takes place as the sketching out of ideas, plots, themes, settings, imagined people, places, things – and can be represented as territory or points in a writingscape. More mapping occurs in creative writing than in any other kind of writing because of the inventiveness of our activities, the vast range of exchanges between our conscious and our unconscious, as Gilles Deleuze and Félix Guattari describe it. We can include among the mapped aspects of what we do such things as:

Word maps, or word clouds which, by juxtaposing and contrasting and collecting single words into a graphic, aim to develop ideas, to build a sense of direction from initial imaginative leaps, to consider perspectives, find possibilities in partial thoughts and observations, even get the first phrases or sentences or lines of a short story or a poem. When physically in front of us as this graphic we see in a word map a not yet formed piece of creative writing – and yet, for some writers the project is entirely there, laid out in those clouds of words.

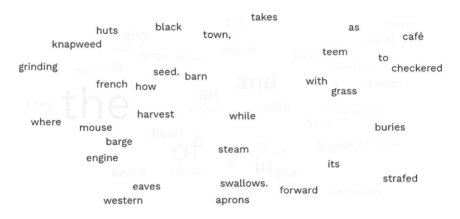

Given the way the human brain works – with cells communicating synaptically, and the nerve cells of the brain's hippocampus linking things – it could be that this graphic depiction of associative words is representative of how our brains are already working; that, in effect, we are creating our own internal word maps.

Mind maps are reminiscent of word maps, but these can be more complete visualizations, organizing information frequently in a hierarchy so that they work as ways of centering your thoughts. In fact, mind maps literally can center information, having one main hub idea, around which others are connected in spokes, prongs, or branches. Mapping this way might also involve symbols, diagrams, and shapes, as well as words, and endeavor to show pathways between one piece of information and another, sometimes guided by route markers (so, for example, the central idea might be 'Climate Change', the route maker on one spoke might say 'Rising Seas' and the prongs at the end of the spoke say 'Erosion', 'Fisheries' and 'Islands'). Mind maps attempt to think graphically so that we are not as reliant on memory to continue to make the connections. Decision-making, brainstorming, and organizing are associated with mind-mapping. Educational consultant Tony Buzan was one of the world's best-known advocates of mind-mapping, publishing *The Mind Map Book* (1993), among many other books.

Spatial maps essentially offer us opportunities to represent a writing project in terms of the location of aspects within it. So, actions, images, characters, events, historical phenomena. Frequently, creative writing can result in an object of some kind, on paper or otherwise, and a spatial map can capture the geometry of such things. Before the advent of digital technologies, generations of readers associated books entirely with tactility, literally with touching a poem or a story. This spatial sense remains because, even if a piece of creative writing is ultimately only in the electronic realm, it has geometry, and within that there are relationships of place and purpose. Traditional examples include the spacing of poetry (concrete poetry being an experiment with linguistic arrangements that extend geometric notions) and the structural properties of many novels, where line breaks, chapters, parts, and sections work as spatial determinants for the shape of a story, the entrance and impact of characters and voices and tones, and the relationship between scenes and summaries that move the novel along.

Roadmaps are found in creative writing, pictorially, but also as lists of potential directions and stopping points. This can be about the content of the work itself or in terms of the techniques of writing. So, a creative writing roadmap can depict locations to be described in a work, and the directions to travel between locations, or it can otherwise describe the relationships between the locations in topographic terms. It can work as a schedule of your writing, or as a plan for getting a work completed. So a roadmap can contain information on what you are going to write about, and about where in the composition you plan to write about it and, perhaps, about why it is something you'll write about. Unlike a word map or a mind map, this could indeed be a technical depiction, relating a plan of composition and a direction and likely arrival point. A roadmap can contain goals and even a timeline – the number of creative writers is substantial who have mentioned recording the number of words they have written in a day, a week, a year. Ernest Hemingway is one well-known notable example (Hemingway, 2019).

Diagrams and Symbols

Diagrammatic, symbolic depictions of creative writing, our working, and our works are mapped in all these ways. What follows cannot necessarily be viewed in a similar vein, given some of it is not necessarily diagrammatic, and some of it is not necessarily symbolic. However, each does also have a relationship to mapping as a learning tool, organizing sets of information:

Descriptive doodles could be considered a somewhat generous inclusion in the list of maps, but the reason for their inclusion is simple: even with the invention of computing, doodles continue to feature in writers' working as examples of conscious and unconscious exploring. Like maps, they are graphic ways of focusing attention. Often, in their case, the focus is on a thought. They too, like maps, are pictorial outlets for feelings, or for not yet fully formed responses to something. Doodles can be evidence of a writer accessing their subconscious as well as the conscious. They are also creative expressions. Exhibitions of doodles as art, much as exhibitions of maps, have been widely held, and there is an interest in the doodles of well-known artists, often to consider if there is evidence of their imaginations to be found in those doodles, much as there are critical studies of the doodles of creative writers (Allen). Doodles are regularly associated with daydreaming, where we might use them to seek our meaning or to consider our interpretation of something or to access a memory.

Character genealogies, or character studies, written out by a novelist, perhaps, or a short story writer, a playwright, or a screenwriter, are included here because in the same way we see happening in geographic mapping their aim is symbolic. Character studies set out context and expectation – much like a map – but their specific purpose is to provide the writer with a grounding for how the character will act, and why. These not uncommon compendiums are our writerly way of setting out what *should* be found; and they offer us a chance to suggest (to ourselves, as writers) what *could* be found but is not. In this way, character studies are individualized by the writers who use them. They are not actual people (even if a character study is based on a real person), but rather are guiding psychological profiles. They require writer and reader interpretation; again, much like maps.

Finally, I include as what we can call 'quasi-maps', **game plans** and **field guides.** Game planning means the setting out of an approach to a creative writing project, which could include themes, subjects, and structures but is largely a strategic outline. A game plan is not a picture of what a project contains as much as it is a way of achieving the goal or goals you set yourself as the writer. Field guides are in some sense 'operational manuals', comprising the kinds of information we collect and arrange to develop and support the authenticity of a work, to give us enough knowledge of things beyond our own lives that we can relate to them or relate things about them, connecting to other lives (readers, audiences) by bringing together our individual knowledge and any knowledge they might have. This is how creative writing works, connecting individual to individual, and while the knowledge we offer in creative writing is not the same kind we find in, say, the sciences or social sciences, it needs to be grounded in congruency – and it is that congruency we map out, in background subjects and pieces of context, in concepts, in points of reference should we need to refer back to what is informing our creative writing project.

Key Features

Whether internal or external maps, whether spatial or word maps or otherwise, all our mapping activities contain main features:

Symbols. Doodles, images, words, and phrases that represent something or someone. The gestures that will give life to these symbols will be the gestures of our writing. But the maps we create to assist us are underpinnings, anchors or guides in the exact same way we use geographic maps when traveling from place to place.

Visualizations and directions. Because writing is inscribing (making words more permanent than they are if merely spoken) and because it is based on action, it is natural that our mapping involves visualizing (notwithstanding words recorded or words accessed by touch). It is natural our mapping also involves suggesting direction because works of creative writing have a starting point and an end point – even when set out graphically in the most open way. We are heading somewhere (often to the conclusion of a piece of writing!) and we started somewhere, however fitfully that start occurred.

Terrain. Mapping involves knowing and depicting terrain, and our creative writing mapping certainly entails that too. In this instance, terrain means the dimensions of our project and what is in it and what is around it. A creative writing project is within this terrain of the cultural and personal influences it contains, and it creates (and we are also creating the terrain of the project as we undertake it). Therefore, a mind map, or a number of doodles, or a spatial map can all show aspects of this terrain.

Relationships and connections. Mapping either explicitly shows connections, such as when it identifies junctions or reveals unbroken patterns in the terrain, or implicitly, such as when it contains references (names, for example) that appear to have similar origins. Writerly mapping is an example of this, in that we gather into maps of all kinds our connection making, bringing together elements of a project or projects. Mapping involves revealing and suggesting relationships. In creative writing, any number of relationships are explored between persons, between places, between events, small and large. Frequently in suggesting connections and in delving into relationships between people and things we create the substance of our works.

Writing in Tom Harper's book *Maps and the 20th Century: Drawing the Line,* Nick Baron proclaims:

> Maps curate our experience of the world as well as guiding our movement through it.
>
> *(Baron, 2016: 239)*

In creative writing, our 'curation' and our 'movement' are frequently the satisfaction we gain and the job we undertake. The labor of creative writing is mapped by these two aspects, to somehow record (for our own purposes or for those who might read or otherwise experience our writing) and to do so by our experiences in the world, our time moving in it and through it.

References

Allen, Graham, 'Shelley as Visual Artist: Doodles, Sketches, Ink Blots, and the Critical Reception of the Visual', *Studies in Romanticism*, 60, no. 3, 2021, pp. 277–306.

Baron, Nick, *Maps and the 20th Century: Drawing the Line*, Tom Harper (ed), London: British Library, 2016.

Biaz, Brooke, *Releasing the Animals,* Parlor: Anderson, 2023.

Brady, Tara, https://www.dailymail.co.uk/news/article-2326630/Notes-diagrams-famous-authors-including-J-K-Rowling-Sylvia-Plath-planned-novels.html (Last Accessed, December 22, 2023).

Burroughs, William, *Junkie*, New York: Ace Books, 1953.

Burroughs, William, *Naked Lunch*, New York: Grove, 1959.

Burroughs, William in Eric Mottram, *William Burroughs: The Algebra of Need*, 1971, London: Marion Boyars, 1977.

Buzan, Tony, *The Mind Map Book*, London: BBC Books, 1993.

Carter, Rita, *Mapping the Mind*, London: Weidenfeld and Nicholson, 1998.

Cendrowski, Mark, 'The Bakersfield Episode', *The Big Bang Theory*, CBS, January 10, 2013.

Deleuze, Gilles and Felix Guattari, *A Thousand Plateaus: Capitalism and Schizophrenia*, trans. Brian Massumi, London: The Athlone Press, 1987.

Harper, Graeme, *Creative Writing Analysis*, London: Routledge, 2023.

Hemingway, Sean, 'Introduction', in Ernest Hemingway, *For Whom the Bell Tolls: The Hemingway Library Edition*, New York: Scriber, 2019, p. xv.

Heritage, Barbara, 'Reading the Writing Desk: Charlotte Brontë's Instruments and Authorial Craft', *Studies in Romanticism*, 60, no. 4, Winter 2021, pp. 503–522.

Kovecses, Zoltan, *Metaphor: A Practical Introduction*, 2nd ed., Oxford: Oxford University Press, 2010.

6

YOUR NAVIGATIONAL VOICE

Natural Insights

'The Basics', a learning network of communities, is a remarkable initiative to build community capacity by engaging and supporting parents of young children or caregivers, in a diverse range of communities. Growing out of the Achievement Gap Initiative (AGI) at Harvard University, it focuses on cognitive skill gaps between children of different racial, ethnic, and parental-education groups, particularly the age ranges from birth to age three. In their book *The Formula* (2019), CEO of The Basics, Ronald Ferguson and journalist Tatsha Robertson include a chapter entitled 'The Navigational Voice in Their Head', in which they say:

> the parent as navigational voice is more than a collection of aphorisms . . . the parental GPS is a map of insights stitched together from lessons the child has learned from their parents about life. It provides a sense of direction that helps the adult achievers navigate their own lives and become fully realized human beings.
>
> *(Ferguson and Robertson, 2019: 270)*

The capacity to seek out and employ navigation is presented here as an educational strategy as well as a means of improving the likelihood of success in life. According to Ron Ferguson and Tatsha Robertson it comes with 'maps', 'insights', 'lessons', a 'sense of direction', and the ability to be 'fully realized'. This natural human capacity is enhanced when we actively recognize it and more actively employ it. That is to say, human beings are not only capable of navigating but the exchanges that occur in childhood – say, between child

DOI: 10.4324/9781003174400-6

and parent – are built around degrees and styles and, most importantly, abilities to navigate.

Ancient mariners voyaged using the stars and the then-known land masses, the appearance of the ocean, and the position of the sun. When mechanical devices were created to assist this navigation, these devices were applied to established human knowledge that informed the using of them. But navigation is not simply based on the external, physical objects we use to assist us. Even in the contemporary world, navigation is not a matter of employing software or artificial intelligence and then heading unthinkingly to your destination. Interpretation happens, you make leaps of faith, routes are considered and reconsidered, even when 'best routes' are offered our minds play a role and our imaginations too. It is to these aspects we can turn, together with the various things involved in physical direction-finding, when considering other guides for navigating in creative writing.

Navigating

The things that assist your navigation of creative writing can be considered in these ways:

Personal (generally). Our individual psychologies naturally impact on everything we do; so, perhaps there is no revelation in saying they impact on our creative writing. However, there is evidence of a distinctiveness to the creative heightening of responses to what is around us, what is happening or has happened to us, and the act of recording these things creatively in writing. Todd Lubart, in Scott Barry Kaufman and James C. Kaufman's *The Psychology of Creative Writing* (2009), remarks:

> Another key feature of creative work is the implication of a state of unusually productive mental flow. Several literary creators, as well as creative people in other fields, have described being in a temporary state of heightened awareness, complete engagement and concentration.
>
> *(Lubart, 2009: 158)*

'Heightened awareness' seems overly adventurous as a guide, if not a little precarious. However, we might argue that creativity is always an activity of precariousness. Certainly, innovation (which is associated with positive creativity) is regarded as precarious in its causing of disruption. Innovation disrupts by creating changes in established practice, or it builds on what exists in a way that advances a need or desire possessed by one human or by many. In these and other ways, the precariousness of heightened awareness *is* a kind of guide. When writing creatively we are heightening written language in some way, if not in style then in content, if not in the writing mechanics then certainly in the intended impact or point of connection with an audience. Not all creative writing is innovative, but all of it is conceivably precarious.

Our own psychology can help us navigate (if we have a degree of comfort with our emotions and behaviors, albeit not always acceptance of them). Our home life, work life, family life all influence us – and while not navigational devices they are the contextual elements within which our writing occurs. We can define these as directing or indicating elements (that is, aspects that produce or influence our response to the world in our writing, or that assist us in writing or that prevent us from writing, or that sustain our writing). Creative writers might not be more attuned to their contexts than any other human beings, but like many creative practitioners those contexts are influential in making our work and in what our work focuses upon.

There are occasions where our efforts are more personally challenging than usual. On that front, one of the enduring discussions in creative writing is indeed that terror called 'writers block'. How actual such a singularly definable condition is, and how pervasive that condition might be bears consideration. It is certainly true that some projects challenge writers to the point where they are unable to write very much, stalled by a lack of ideas, or a lack of technical prowess to solve a problem, or lack of motivation that seems borne on their limited enthusiasm for spending the time and energy. One thing is certain, a block of this kind relates to a personal, psychological condition and while not a guide, as such, it is a reminder that writing involves action and movement and that there is always context to be discovered about why that movement has ceased.

Cultural. The cultural circumstances – contemporary and historic – in which we are writing clearly inform each of us. Though we filter these through our minds, we also ground our literary understanding in terms of nation or region, and through the language we use, and according to the city we live in, in relation to the neighborhood, and according to whether we were born locally or not. We have a sense of contemporary writing style based on commonsense communication between existing groups of people, and we relate conditions of life that are contemporary references to (and influenced by) our associated sense of race and gender, sexuality and able-bodiedness, and by our economic position in a society.

Simply, then, we write within cultural circumstances that vary in strength and influence. We can be part of a dominant cultural narrative or situated outside of it. We can be writing as participants in the continuation and maintenance of the mainstream, or we can be writing in opposition to it. A general sense of where we are situated can act as a backdrop to what and how we write, or it can be the primary driving factor behind our writing. Expressly, wider cultural influence is not manifest in us evenly, it is determined by our interaction with that around us as individuals and in closer social groups – family friends. Mapping this, having a personal sense of this, helps to guide our writing.

Educational (specifically) Formal educational guidance is provided for us by institutions offering classes and courses. Informal education we undertake largely outside those institutions, on our own, and it varies according to familial and community influences. Creative writing education, in the literate cultures where it exists, has been located somewhere between these two positions. Celebrating personal talent, and valuing individualism in creative writing we have tended not to expect formal education in it (and certainly not to require that, as we might in some fields of human endeavor – medicine and engineering being two obvious ones, where professional accreditation validates expertise). Informal education has featured in the biographies of writers, the role of fortuitous discovery, and the ambience of their individual lives, often of a zeal, and of an inventiveness that exceeds the ordinary.

Creative practitioners have been associated with this kind of extraordinariness, a transcendence of the day-to-day, an ability to see beyond what appear to be invariable rules and constraints. Therefore, in general ordinary education has not often been a major part of a creative writer's story, certainly not part of one viewed as successful. And yet, formal education in creative writing has long been around – from that happening in the ancient universities of India, Italy, Morocco, England, Spain, and Egypt to that in the contemporary universities, now across almost the entire world.

Historically, formal education in creative writing has grown exponentially since the mid-20th century – in some countries more than others. This has happened for various reasons. In some instances it is due to its inclusion in government programs focused on improving national literacy. In the USA, for example, Deborah Brandt explores this in her well-known book *Literacy in American Lives* (2001):

> Jordan Grant, educated in segregated schools in Arkansas and Tennessee during the 1950s and early 1960s, remembered a major poetry unit in high school that began with extensive lessons on the conventional forms and technical vocabulary of poetry. Next, students designed and produced book covers. After that, they filled their books with five or six poems by white poets, five or six poems by black poets, and then, in the back of the book, a number of their own poems in the different forms they had studied. Younger people whom I interviewed, those born from the late 1960s onward, tended to remember more creative writing assigned, especially in the early grades.
>
> *(Brandt, 2001: 164)*

In other instances, the growth in creative writing education rode on the back of wider explorations of creativity, from early years education right into college education. Further, and largely in colleges, in the development of immersion in creative writing practice for those seeking to go on to write professionally. Occasionally, in the connection with English language learning in countries where English is not a first language. In genre activities around particular creative industries, such as film production or the theater. In personal therapies and in community development. In the pursuit of exploring the findings of other disciplines in the social sciences and the sciences and more. Education in creative writing – whether formal or informal – creates its own trace, its own conditions of engagement that provide us, as creative writers, with touchpoints and signposts to what we are doing.

Experiential (generally). We might or might not know exactly where an idea comes from that launches our latest creative writing project. We might or might not know how our experiences direct and inform where and what and how a poem investigates an observation or how a screenplay creates scenes. But we do know that our experiences, generally, play a role, as logically they would. Many a time a teacher of creative writing will encourage their students to 'write what you know' (an expression heard often enough in creative writing teaching to be cliché) or to 'base what you write on a personal event' – and the aim is to encourage those learning creative writing to find in their own experience something meaningful and interesting enough to stimulate and sustain their work. An experience, however, does not need to be the subject of your writing to be influential. Creative writing is content, and form, and structure, and voice, pace and viewpoint, and more – and each of these things, each element of technique, and of what you write about can potentially take something from your experiences in the world. Experiential guidance might be akin to self-awareness, or to a sense of understanding the context of things that have happened or that are happening around you.

All these things provide guides of some kind and in some way for our practice and for the critical understanding we bring to it. In that respect, all can, of course, be a point of reference for how we understand our work and the work of other writers. More practically, each of these areas of influence can be explored by us to better understand how we write and why we write and in what ways we go about writing. Navigation involves interpretation and how we interpret is as significant as what we interpret.

Creative writing isn't fixed primarily on information exchange (as is scientific writing, for instance), and it is not primarily about engaging the reader or audience in a point of view that is to the benefit of the writer (as is advertising, where the goal, whether for profit or not-for-profit is largely to convince someone of something). Works of creative writing are not always attempting to convince anyone of anything – more commonly only to present, or observe or speculate or consider. Not every work of creative writing is meant to be immediately understood; as is essential with, say, written warnings, alerts and directives, which would be useless if they were not preemptory and straightforward. And works of creative writing are not always meant to be diverting, even if they are sometimes largely for entertainment; that is, they can also be contemplative and sober, even at times severe. What we choose to write about creatively, and how we choose to do it, ultimately relies on what we find valuable in the work that we do.

Other Navigational Influences

Considering these influences, other guides to creative writing practically come in many forms:

Other disciplines. Creative writers consider and employ knowledge across the entirety of human life. In the academic world, this knowledge is organized in disciplinary groupings – represented by university departments and the like – in an effort to focus attention and effort on research and teaching in these defined types and varieties of knowledge. Creative writing, over time, has found itself mostly in the close company of the study of Literature, sometimes in the company of Linguistics or Languages, further in the company of Media, Film, Theater, and sometimes associated with the study of Music or the creating of Leisure Software. These academic groupings suggest these are cognate subjects, either related to creative writing because they help us understand it (in terms of the study of Literature or Language) or related to it because within these areas of human activity creative writing occurs or is a prevalent aspect (such as screenwriting in the exploration of film or songwriting in the study of music). These kinds of knowledge relationships provide guidance of a direct and associative kind built around creative-critical thinking and our creative action, where we closely consider what is created as much as go about creating it.

However, the navigational guides we find in the academic world, as well as the knowledge we find in the wider world, go beyond areas closely associated with creative writing. Both literally and figuratively, other types and wider areas of knowledge offer us content for our writing, acting as a source of information and observations as well as providing impetus for our ideas and stimulating our imaginations. Creative writing content therefore is found in any number of places. And it is not only content we're seeking or able to employ. Such disciplinary guides also offer us illustrations of processes, of ways of seeing things and of ways of analyzing.

These navigational guides are, in effect, examples of the questions humans ask, and of what humans find interesting or challenging, or of how humans see connections in their knowledge and understanding. Other disciplines can guide us by showing (a) the shapes of knowledge – how we put it in order, and suggest connections between one thing and another, (b) the relationships between types and styles of knowledge, (c) the ways we think of aspects of our knowledge, and (d) how we value certain kinds of knowledge. We can even use these elements to help us imagine a structure for a piece of creative writing – again, literally or figuratively. More or less, this means that because our organizing of knowledge reflects how we view what we understand, and how we go about putting it into an order to improve and indicate our comprehension, it also acts as a guide.

Sometimes our organizing of knowledge can be a visual guide. For example, the way Chemistry constructs a formula could explain to us, figuratively, the plot of a novel. Or the way Architecture sees a building might explain the relationship between the patterns seen in a poem. Or the way Mathematics represents the components of an equation could be a visual guide to how we construct a short story:

$$D = \sqrt{(x_1 - x_2) + (y_1 - y_2)}$$

An unlikely but possible figurative example, with D equaling how far the story will travel from its opening to its conclusion (in terms of story or in terms of length) and the X and Y representing two groups of things that occur in the story. Although it is improbable that many creative writers would use such a mathematical model the visual representation of how we make something 'add up' is one example of how we reveal and represent knowledge. It also shows how someone working in mathematics might start out with an idea and come to some kind of conclusion. We observe these organizational actions in the world, and much of what we do is impacted upon by this – take the way in which knowing the structure and system of a grocery store in the Western world impacts our understanding of where we get what we eat.

Of course, while incorporating the structures and systems fundamental to writing, creative writing is empowered by the liveliness and fluidity of our imaginations. It is not that those engaged with other kinds of knowledge, other kinds of writing, or generally in other kinds of communication fail to use their imaginations or, worse still, that they are not able to be imaginative at all. Rather, it is that creative writing involves an enhanced facility for movement between thoughts and feelings, between different types and conditions of knowledge, between an appeal to ourselves, undertaking writing that means something to us, and a reach out to others. Other disciplines of knowledge influence this and provide models for how we organize and present our writing.

Spatial indicators. The human world is based on forms of space and types of spatial organization. We see this in the construction of our homes, and in the human places through which we travel. Architecture adds style to this, practicality produces engagement. We consider space a guide to such things as ownership, or as part of a system of necessary organization so that our world functions in a commonsense, workable way. When we locate things in the human world, we take into account such aspects as access, impact, convenience, or association (that is, putting things where they allow or encourage a relationship between things – a neighborhood and a park, for example).

Nature also presents us with forms of space and types of spatial organization. We have long attempted to fathom this, and to work with it and control or adjust it to suit ourselves. These spatial indicators are so commonplace that while we don't consciously and continuously examine them, they do impact upon our sense of where we are and why we are here. They send signals to us about the type of experience we're having and the reasons we are having it.

Writing, likewise, is based on organizing space. At the most basic level the gaps between words, and the size and shape of letters, are spatial indictors. In the English language, the capitalization of a word or the inclusion of an ellipsis . . . both tell us something about what and how something is being said. Spatial indicators are instructive in creative writing, partly because writing uses these kinds of basic communication codes. But spatial indicators are also examples of arrangement and ordering in our world – whether by ourselves or by nature. We therefore find in combining the fluidity of our imaginations and the systematized way writing works a need to use spatial indicators – and we draw them often from the human and natural worlds to shape and configure what we do.

Creative writing in this shaping and configuring appeals to us in the same way the organizing of space appeals to us. Disorder and chaos are considered troublesome, perhaps dangerous, often unfathomable, or unintelligible. Creative writers have occasionally traveled near to these things in the interest of literary experiment. But some kind of order has proven more appealing – to writers and, it appears, also to readers and audiences. We are therefore guided in our creative writing by the ordering of space we see in the world. This might be visual messaging – the appearance of a city block – or it might be the indications we receive from how things occur (for example, the relationship between the shore and the ocean as the tide turns, changing the space each occupies).

Temporal indicators. Philosopher Henri Bergson famously suggested time is not so much a scientific subject as a philosophic one. His contemporary, physicist Albert Einstein, approached it as a scientific one. Their consequent disagreement is considered in Jimena Canales book *The Physicist and the Philosopher: Einstein, Bergson, and the Debate That Changed Our Understanding of Time* (Canales, 2016) Either way, time is a definer of much in our lives, and it creates a pattern that is discernible and obvious – on the surface, at least. Beneath the surface, our memories offer insights, bridging present and past and creating a version of time we might consider to be more like Bergson's than Einstein's. 'Clock time' is less the time we refer to when we refer to memories than the time of 'duration' (as Bergson named it), which is not so much measurable as it is experienced.

Simple temporal indicators of the scientific kind, that inform our creative writing, include the chronology of events and the length of our days and weeks. We construct our works of creative writing based on this understanding – to the extent of using this common, scientific understanding of time to order narratives, or the sequences of events in a story, or the amount of time it takes to read a sentence or a line, or the length of dialogue in a play, or the way a scene in a screenplay relates the journey of a character from one location to another.

Temporal indicators more in line with Bergson's notion of time can be found in how in creative writing we use flashback and flashforward (more formally called 'analepsis' and 'prolepsis'). We do so to create a sense of relation and association between past, present, and future. Bergson also questions ideas about causation, suggesting that while time might consist of moments there is not a standard way in which one moment causes another but, rather, that moments exist in multiplicity, and are diverse. According to Bergson, if we stop things still to measure them we change them, and therefore don't really come to understand them accurately at all.

This idea of time being continuous and these Bergsonian challenges to the idea of causation remind us of forms of creative writing (some poetry, perhaps, some forms of dramatic writing) where the temporal indicators are more those of what Bergson calls 'duration' (the continuous flow of consciousness where what the writer is doing is presenting something going on in that continuous flow, some moments that are not separated out from the rest but are distinct from what is occurring around them).

Patterns (your life). Creative writing is rarely anyone's sole occupation. Even some of the world's most well-known writers have had lives beyond their writing, and these lives influenced and informed their work. Brief examples include the Tanzanian-born Abdulrazak Gurnah, who was employed as a Professor of English and Postcolonial Literatures, and American poet Wallace Stevens (1879–1955) who worked most of his life as an insurance company executive. Toni Morisson, author of *Song of Solomon* (1977), among other notable works, was teaching at Howard University when she first began to write in earnest, and then worked in book publishing, (at first in the textbook division of Random House), before publishing her first novel at age 39. Novelist and short story writer Haruki Murakami ran a jazz club called Peter Cat, in the Sendagaya neighborhood of Tokyo, while writing his first novels, *Hear the Wind Sing* (1979) and *Pinball, 1973* (1980). Numerous other writers began their working lives in other jobs before becoming full-time creative writers: science fiction writer, Octavia E. Butler, as a dishwasher and telemarketer; poet Philip Larkin as a librarian.

We are guided in our creative writing by our own lives; and, if those lives involve occupations other than being a creative writer then clearly the pattern, shape, and rhythm of those occupations are going to influence us and the things that we write. Our own lives can provide content for our work (of course) and they can provide models of how something might be done or viewed or put in context. So, we personalize our creative writing, consciously and unconsciously, and in doing so we're establishing not only the uniqueness of what we do (through this personalization) but also the quality we find in works of creative writing, whereby they connect one human experience (the writer's) with that of others (the reader or audience). This is a quality of creative writing that exists regardless of the subject matter or theme. It is as much an expectation as it is a technique, grounded in the ideal of human creativity, of bonding, and sharing. Even if we employ artificial intelligence to generate or assist our writing or draw on older technologies that simply suggest or correct or stimulate words and ideas, it is the humanness of the activity that drives creative writing – that of the writer and that of those who receive the writing.

Patterns (other lives). Creative writers often actively observe others – and, indeed, we find numerous examples of writerly research techniques that involve writers going places or immersing themselves in situations in the interest of generating or simply observing experiences, about which they write. This can be a direct patterning of our writing activities. We also frequently consider a writer's peopled day-to-day environments creating observable guides to the work they produce, and literary critics have often drawn on such evidence to consider both the declared and undeclared origins, style and character of a particular writer's works.

But the lives of others also provide a guide as a form of general knowledge, that can be historical as much as it can be contemporary. We are influenced by what we know of human lives, whether we actively study or observe them or not. Creative writing, in encouraging a fluid engagement with the world around us, and the records of the world past, and speculations on a world of the future, encourages us to imagine lives beyond our own and endeavor to relate to them. This is part of our patterning of the relationship between our individual writerly activities and the reader or audience that will encounter our writing. It is, in effect, a form of empathy, of the kind mentioned by Heidi Maibom in her book *The Space Between: How Empathy Really Works* (2022). Maibom writes:

> a conscious mind is always *somewhere*. It is always the mind of a situated creature that needs to survive. But although we cannot adopt a view from nowhere, we can adopt many different perspectives successively and thereby come to a more nuanced way of seeing the world.
>
> *(Maibom, 2022: 35)*

Maibom's 'situated creature' is a creative writer. We are always located somewhere, our guides being that which is around us, and our experiences, and our opinions and ideas and ideals and emotions. And yet, writing asks us to create something of relative permanence, an etched representation of what would otherwise have been unsaid or said verbally and then largely would have disappeared. In doing so, writing relies on the guide of the world we see and imagine and have experienced. The lives of others become part of our writing whether we acknowledge it or not. We're creating in 'the space between' – between our individual life and the lives of others. Ancient mariners navigated using the stars and the then known land masses, the appearance of the ocean and the position of the sun; but all navigation involves interpretation, leaps of faith, and the influence of our imaginations. As creative writers, we are guided by our individual psychology, by culture, by our education, and by our experiences. Other areas of human knowledge provide content for our writing, but also models of structure and of relationships between what is known and what is not known. Our understanding of space and of time influence our way of using the tools of writing – and act as indicators of systems of measurement and organization, conditions that are all around us, and that impact our practice of writing as much as they create the form of the world in which we live. We live according to a pattern of our own life, and often in sight of, and certainly aware of, the patterns of the lives of others – some of whom, we might hope, will become the readers or audiences for our finished creative writing. A developed awareness of these aspects within us and around us is not impossible – even for the new creative writer, who might be heavily focused on the techniques of writing that are not yet second nature. The challenge here is not about whether any of us has the ability to write creatively; but, more so, about whether we give ourselves the best possible chance of succeeding in our work by drawing on the guides that are within and around us.

References

Brandt, Deborah, *Literacy in American Lives*, Cambridge: Cambridge University Press, 2001.

Canales, Jimena, *The Physicist and the Philosopher: Einstein, Bergon and the Debate that Changed the Understanding of Time*, Princeton: Princeton University Press, 2016.

Ferguson, Ronald F. and Tatsha Robertson, *The Formula: Unlocking the Secrets of Raising Highly Successful Children*, Dallas: BenBella Books, 2019.

Lubart, Todd, 'In Search of the Writer's Creative Process', in *The Psychology of Creative Writing*, Scott Barry Kaufman and James C. Kaufman (eds), Cambridge: Cambridge University Press, 2009, pp. 149–165.

Maibom, Heidi, *The Space Between: How Empathy Really Works*, New York: Oxford University Press, 2022.

Morrison, Toni, *Song of Solomon*, New York: Alfred A. Knopf, 1977.

Murakami, Haruki, *Hear the Wind Sing*, Tokyo: Kodansha, 1979.

Murakami, Haruki, *Pinball, 1973*, Tokyo: Kodansha, 1980.

7
MOBILITY

Jean-Dominique Bauby

Simple observation shows creative writing involves progress. Written work done, things created (books, texts) are seemingly immobile, although as the world changes around them they too in some manner move when they are re-visited, reinterpreted, renewed by those changing conditions; they change too, some might argue, when viewed through different lenses, from different criti-cal viewpoints, under varying cultural conditions, and according to individual backgrounds. But at the basic level of its physical presence, **the written** is an object, while **writing** involves mobility progress. The sweep of a hand, the ac-cumulation of letters typed, or the curl of a letter written out:

When thinking about, and then undertaking a piece of creative writing we are therefore always engaged with types of mobility, with progress, and with some style, condition, reason, and regard for progress.

The basic task of getting marks to appear on a page (or, most likely today, notations on a screen) has history as a fascinatingly ancient practice, that reminds us that the primary aim of most writing is to put in place some-thing that can be present and can communicate and can, in the case of crea-tive writing, entertain as well as enlighten and enrich others, even when the writer is no longer present. This artisan aspect of creative writing – which

DOI: 10.4324/9781003174400-7

has generated discussions of craft broadening to be defined as 'skill' and 'technique' but which is still primarily referring to artisanal action – is about the physical actions we undertake. If we ever wonder how relevant our consideration of movement in creative writing happens to be, we can think about Jean-Dominique Bauby, and his remarkable writing of his memoir, *The Diving Bell and The Butterfly* (1998).

> Enough rambling. My main task now is to compose the first of these bedridden travel notes so that I shall be ready when my publisher's emissary arrives to take my dictation, letter by letter. In my head I churn over every sentence ten times, delete a word, add an adjective, and learn my text by heart, paragraph by paragraph.
>
> *(Bauby, 1998: 5)*

Jean-Dominique Bauby was the editor of French *Elle* magazine when, at the age of 43, he had a stroke that resulted in him suffering locked-in syndrome (a condition of almost complete paralysis except, typically, in which the patient is able to blink). His memoir is about his life before and after his stroke, as well as a series of dreams, childhood memories, memories of his working life, travel, relationships, life in the hospital, visits from friends, medical procedures, flashes of history and thoughts about the culture and people he knows or things he could do, family, imagined life as a soldier or cyclist or visitor to places he has not yet been. It is a memorable work, in its subject and in its themes. Much that is discussed about it, however, begins with the ways Bauby composed the work by blinking his left eye. For two months, three hours a day, seven days a week the author progressed his book this way – and it is this framing of the memoir in those conditions of its writing that most drives the discussion of Bauby's memoir.

Jean-Dominique Bauby's memoir writing is a story of resilience beyond the ordinary, a striking example of the human spirit. In its critical reception it is also the story of how we associate any kind of writing with a certain kind of progress. Dutch artist M.C. Escher's well-known lithograph entitled 'Drawing Hands' (1948) - depicting two hands drawing each other - could be viewed as much about writing as it is about drawing. In a similar vein are the ever popular depictions of the quill, the ink pot and the typewriter seen on the covers of many creative writing books – each awaiting the hands that will use them and bring them to life. These drawings suggest change, they await proceeding. We view them with expectation.

Keyboards, pencils, and nibs all suggest (in their appearance and their precise design) the movements that can and must occur in order for us to write, even though we know writing might be done by voice recording or, in the case of Jean-Dominique Bauby, blinking, or by arrangement of stones on the ground, for that matter, or with white smoke blown from small aircraft (by oil injected onto a hot engine manifold, incidentally). But it is the physicality, the need for progress, that is prominent and, perhaps, reflective of expectation that the topics, observations, characters, images, discussions, going on with a piece of creative writing will also move in some way. The boilerplate notion of a piece of writing having a beginning, middle, and end is a reference to progress. The conditions of poetic cadence and tempo are progressive. The transitions between one scene and another in a screenplay only help to emphasize that an entire film script is made up of progression: characters in and out of frame, cameras moving, sounds on and off, constant rolling forward. Finally, Samuel Beckett's *Waiting for Godot*, so often described as a play 'in which nothing happens', reminds us of our expectation of progress, while at the same time (or in contrast, perhaps) challenging the idea that without someone providing it beyond ourselves we have no actual direction and, therefore, potentially no meaning.

Creative writing is progress, and we undertake it and navigate it by understanding that progress, its nature, and its variety, along with the things we encounter on the way and methods by which those movements result in experience of things we imagined exploring and things we did not imagine until we began to write.

Toward

The basic movements we're talking about are those involved in inscribing, typing, etching, making a mark. Writing almost always involves some kind of hand and eye movement – it is physical in that simple sense. We might recall any number of scenes – in your own life or in the popular media – where the proctor of an old school examination calls 'Pencils down!' into a dusty, cavernous school hall, full of students in checkered school uniforms, and that venerable hall instantly fills with the sound of pencils hitting wooden desktops. There's an echoic recognition of this for us all – even if we haven't personally experienced it – because writing is an action, and as that proctor strolls out, grey face turning one way and then the other, a slight drag in her left foot perhaps (from an old equestrian injury), a pencil of her own being beaten on her left palm, a curl in a luxuriant brow, lips pursed, we know that if hands are still, shoulders back, jaws steady, eyes fixed forward, then no writing is happening.

A compass can certainly assist in determining a location, regardless of whether you are progressing toward it or standing still. But it is in traveling, in journeying, in making progress that compasses more frequently are employed. The magnetic compass is itself constantly moving, as if to suggest this possibility – a fact novelist Jerzy Kosiński, author of such works as *The Painted Bird* (1965) and *Being There* (1971) observed: 'I always have a sense of trembling, but so does a compass, after all' (Kosiński, 1972: 196). All writing is not unlike this, and *creative* writing is always this way: expectant.

In literate cultures, we conjecture and contemplate, discover, explain, and imagine – all with the option of writing things down. This is itself a sense of trembling, as Kosiński calls it, where every observation, every thought, every feeling, every unearthed or imagined thing or event can potentially become a written thing. With creative writing even more so because the imperative for all creative writers is to give voice to the imagination, which is dynamic (being untethered by structure or system or time or place), and therefore always moving.

Progress, then. And we seek it as creative writers, and creative writing comes about because of it and writing, because of its graphic origins, and because all else that relates to it comes from those origins, and because when we envisage it, or learn it, or think of it, or wonder on the tools we might use to do it, or compare it with other forms of communication (such as speaking), or reference its definition as a 'set of graphic symbols' or ponder what we mean when we call someone 'a creative writer' – because of *all* this, somewhere there exists in our minds a pictorial image of what we meaning by writing:

So, progress. But what elements are there in progress that we need to consider – much as if, with magnetic compass in hand, we have set out to make our way to a point ahead?

In our case that arrival point is the place where the work we are writing feels complete; or, where we are satisfied we have achieved what we want to achieve with a particular project. Considering our progress, then, involves a range of aspects:

Speed. Every creative writing project has its own pace. Compositional speed is not only how quickly we can type or scrawl, but also how quickly we can ideate and relate one component of our thinking and of imagining to another component and another . . . and another. Speed of progress in creative writing is particularly influenced by this imagination-intellect exchange (how we might project from our memories, which is one kind of imagining, or make from speculative idea, which is another kind of imagining, or reconfigure what we observe into an alternative scenario, an alternative reality, which is another kind of imagining). Experienced creative writers may have a sense of how fast they create their works – borne on the back of that experience. This might give greater confidence in the composition activities they undertake. However, even the most experienced writer finds pace difficult to predict. Therefore, one of our most significant considerations on any creative compositional journey can be our tolerance of the speed or pace of our writing.

Our tolerance of this writing speed or rate (we each bring our own psychology to this consideration) is borne on an often anecdotal or cultural logic. That is, we expect a poem to take less time to write than a novel – simply because logic related to the number of words commonly involved suggests that it should. But the interaction of the imagination and intellect, the speculative, inventive intentions of the creative, and the mechanics of writing are variable. So we need to be open to a range of possibilities. Creative writing is often based on periods of acceleration. At other times it involves all but stasis. The mechanics of putting things 'on paper' may not be happening, even if the thoughts and imagining that inform it are happening. We frequently find what we do as writers features alternations of movement, forward and back, and sideways – ideas or conjectures taking the writer somewhere parallel or peripheral yet important, notions of a true north informing us, revision and editing taking up back to previous places in our work. In figurative ways, we leap, we prop, we run, we walk, we look side to side. In other words, we progress in both linear and non-linear ways, and this produces a sense of speed (or lack of), and knowing this, and anticipating this, and working with this is a strength we can develop as creative writers.

Motion. We can think of this in simple terms as the actions of changing a position. So 'being in motion' could mean actions of writing in any sense. Writing a poem could be the motions of researching a topic, drafting some ideas, reading lines aloud. While speed or pace is about compositional velocity, motion is about creative and critical inclination and impulse. We create motion by actively harnessing how we view a creative writing project, what thoughts and feelings inform it and how these initiate and then potentially evolve; and how these elements relate to the meaning of the work we're doing. It is not coincidence that the word 'motion' can also refer to a formal proposal in a meeting. A motion is a statement of interest and intent, frequently with a suggestion of the outcome or outcomes of doing the thing proposed. Creative writing is not unlike that: we present a 'motion' as writers of things we think, imagine, believe, have observed, or speculate might happen. We communicate by active exploration – motioning, in two senses.

Rhythm. Our progress in a project, and in our writing generally, has a rhythm. It is likely a rhythm based on the tempo of our daily life or, in some instances, on the decision-making process we have gone through in order to undertake some creative writing. For instance, the person who is paid to work full time on their creative writing is likely to have a different measure to their creative writing than the person who is fitting it in around other work. Most creative writers are in the latter category and therefore understanding our individual rhythms becomes a significant aspect of being able to complete a project. Rhythm refers to a pattern – and it is one of the colloquial touchpoints for any number of creative writing instruction books, that say such things as (and these have become common in the genre): 'find a time to write each day' or 'write at the same hour each day' or 'designate time to write'. None of these things is, in essence, incorrect. But each is not quite getting to the reality of creative writing. That is, these comments are referring to a rhythm – the flow, the fluctuations – and, understanding your rhythm, establishing and supporting your rhythm, and using your understanding of your rhythm provides an underpinning for what you are attempting, even if the challenges of you finding time to write are considerable. The world is based on patterns and interrelations, whether in seasons or lifecycles, whether in the heartbeats of creatures or in the visual condition of landscapes, and discovering and using the beat of creative writing to make progress is as natural as these things.

Direction. A creative writing project has directional characteristics – and those characteristics can be defined by *how* those directions are pursued, *how many* directions there might be, and how those directions are *situated in relation to other points* in the journey. Certainly, a project (and its writer) can be heading toward a conclusion – a point at which the project is complete or abandoned (as determined by the writer; perhaps also as determined by a deadline, from a publisher, a creative writing teacher or by a friend or family member). But, we can also be headed toward numerous locations along the way – locations that form or represent waystations and turning points. Progress might be determined by reaching those locations; or, more frequently, by reaching those locations, determining the success of the arrival (a plot junction realized, a rhythmic sequence completed, a revelation made) and moving on to another point in the direction of a perceived destination. Were we to literally have a magnetic compass in hand, the points on the way would be sited against the eventual destination, which would remain relevant (moving needle assisting us to keep that arrival site in focus). In reality, creative writing directions work differently to this, and it is not infrequent that a destination is general, not inevitable, and it is the direction-finding that benefits from our figurative compass, helping us keep in mind locations reached along the way, and suggesting an eventual outcome or arrival point, without that being immutably in place.

Distance. At its simplest creative writing would appear to be defined by lengths of time and lengths of text. Time to do it – measured from start to finish – and what is created – measured by the visible evidence of having done it (in a large part, the writing, or text created). But distance is, in fact, a measurement of how much space or ground is covered.

A creative writing project can cover relatively little physical space but a considerable amount of emotional, intellectual, or observational space. We could play with equations about this, if we were mathematically inclined, producing a representation of physical length multiplied by intellectual or emotional or contextual (for example, historical or cultural) depth explored. The point of such an equation might be questionable. But the notion of it is useful in pointing to how, when we are writing creatively, elements interact.

Some creative writing travels a physical distance (in content, and/or in number of words) but relatively little emotional or contextual distance. Considering this gives us an opportunity to be comfortable with expectations and to quarry our intentions, so that we can track how far we are traveling – in every sense of what distance can mean.

Impulse. Progress involves a motivating force, an urge or a desire. A strong impulse to write something might not necessarily mean we will have the knowledge or the understanding to write it – nor that the impulse will be strong enough to maintain you through a lengthy period of composition. That balance (perhaps again, inputs for an equation attractive to the mathematically inclined) could be strength of impulse multiplied by length of effort required. A lack of progress could indicate the impulse to write a particular piece was not strong enough in the first place; or, that the direction taken was wrong (leading you to be stalled – neither where you want to go nor pleased with where you are) or that you had the impulse but not the knowledge to travel further. Progress, then, is linked to strength of impulse, support for that impulse (that is, knowledge, understanding, or experience), and the success of the directions taken.

Momentum. We can judge and assess our writing momentum (how much it has, that is). Some of this judgment is the result of our established expectations – expectations based on our history of our momentum in undertaking previous writing projects, their perceived rhythm and speed and the force behind or in front of those projects. Force, scientifically speaking, is the external action that pushes or pulls a thing (in our case, a piece of creative writing). Perhaps in your case, that force is the pulling action of a desire to say something or the aim of completing a project for a publication or an event or a presentation or perhaps it is the pushing action of an assignment set for your creative writing class. Our momentum will relate to our individual psychology, our experience, and our intentions, and to external encouragement, obligation, or request. So, for two examples: (1) you want to write a story about a childhood experience to share one day with your niece; (2) a colleague asks for a poem for a publication celebrating an upcoming event.

Immobility. We are able to become more mobile when we are more supple, more exercised, more adaptable, more resilient. Building on this corporeal metaphor, we could say that when we are more exercised the pain is less and the pleasure greater. Athletes might offer some insight into this. In creative writing, a higher degree of writerly mobility tends to be associated with having practiced the activities of creative writing for longer, and in more ways, learning not only the techniques of writing but also experiencing the likely writing scenarios and results that emerge from our actions. We become resilient through familiarity, harnessing techniques to overcome difficulties that emerge in writing, and having alternative. approaches available to us when aspects of the writing are not working, and we not only need technique to overcome them but an ability to recognize productive alternatives.

Needless to say, mobility can also be associated with inconsistency and disorder. So the actions of creative writing, our knowledge and our skills, eventually need to inform a writer knowing when a phrase, a line, or an entire work of creative writing is at the point of being fixed on the page. Not that the works of creative writing cannot be interpreted and reinterpreted by different people, and over time. Simply, that in practical terms creative writers need to achieve a sense in which progress on any writing project involves both mobility and immobility: the capacity to decide on when a piece of creative writing is complete.

Transport. In a consideration of progress of our creative writing, physical things – a poem, a novel, a screenplay, for example – transport our imaginative conjectures, our thoughts, our observations, in our pursuit of putting these on paper (referring to the longevity of writing over spoken words, which tend to be commonly ephemeral). The ways and means by which a thing emerges and becomes an identifiable result of our writing is an indicator of our progress. For centuries before the invention of the computer – more accurately, the specific invention of word processing software – the transporting of these results of our imagining, our thinking, our observing was manifest in paper trails. A multitude of writers' manuscripts, notes, diary entries and correspondence preserved over time alert us to the physicality of writing (that is, to our making literary things). Some of this evidence has continued to be created; but, for the majority of creative writers today work in progress is electronic and therefore intangible. For many contemporary creative writers, the 'transportation' of their writerly artistry never leaves this electronic world, being sent out as digital books or interactive electronic experiences, as games, or as guides for other artforms (in some cases, as they have long been – in the case of play scripts, for example).

What is striking about considering the things creative writers produce, and the long tradition of valuing these objects not only as what I have called here transport for imaginative ideas and feelings and observations but as wonderful aesthetic items, is that we have both embraced and sometimes felt uncomfortable with the shift from solid objects to digital representations, from paper to keystrokes displayed on a computer screen. We appear to value the aesthetic worth of creative writing in its physical form, the way it appears not only as the words it involves, the writerly forms and shapes it takes, but as the forms and shapes and colors and textures, even the aromas, of the containers we have historically created for it. So, we look at the industrial appearance of a printed shooting script for a film and it tells us a story of that film's creation, the labor of it and the material presence of it. We are attracted to book covers. Over generations, much attention has been paid by artists and graphic designers to the relationship between the cover of a book of poems or a novel and the words within. The electronic world has changed a great deal of this, but we continue to value the physicality of how creative writing is brought to us, the shapes and styles of that 'transport', and its sensory appeal.

Tracking and Tracing Creative Writing

Just as we have heard in the case of Ernest Hemingway (p.53, this volume), progress in creative writing has long been trackable and tracked by creative writers. Doing this appears to represent the desire of countless writers to maintain awareness of what is their solitary and shifting human activity. This desire comes about because creative writing is most often a practice that goes unobserved by others, so that the only immediate sounding board for knowing if we are making progress is ourselves. Ours is a practice too that doesn't necessarily move in a linear way, from start to finish, so how progress is measured and traced often involves an awareness of what kinds of mobility we are observing. We commonly find writers mentioning time spent and words written, considering these things within the context of their physical and their psychological engagement, and referring to the life (and other work) that is happening around them. Sometimes they go as far as to track and trace their writing in a way not too far removed from arithmetic.

John Steinbeck, author of *The Grapes of Wrath* (1939) and *East of Eden* (1952), among other works, comments:

> Now let me give you the benefit of my experience in facing 400 pages of blank stock—the appalling stuff that must be filled. I know that no one really wants the benefit of anyone's experience which is probably why it is so freely offered. But the following are some of the things I have had to do to keep from going nuts.

Abandon the idea that you are ever going to finish. Lose track of the 400 pages and write just one page for each day; it helps. Then when it gets finished, you are always surprised.

(Steinbeck, 1975)

Canadian short story writer, Alice Munro, reports similarly on her personal 'quota of pages' and on time spent:

I write every morning, seven days a week. I write starting about eight o'clock and finish up around eleven. Then I do other things the rest of the day, unless I do my final draft or something that I want to keep working on then I'll work all day with little breaks

(Munro, 1994: 260)

I am so compulsive that I have a quota of pages. If I know that I am going somewhere on a certain day I will try to get those extra pages done ahead of time. That's so compulsive, it's awful. But I don't get too far behind, it's as if I could lose it somehow.

(Munro, 1994: 261)

Author of *The Kite Runner* (2003) Khaled Hosseini, refers to 'sequestering' himself, but also mentions a pattern of writing and taking breaks, which ultimately results in '2–3 pages' each day:

Do you have any unusual rituals in your writing process?
   I write while my kids are at school and the house is quiet. I sequester myself in my office with mug of coffee and computer. I can't listen to music when I write, though I have tried. I pace a lot. Keep the shades drawn. I take brief breaks from writing, 2–3 minutes, by strumming badly on a guitar. I try to get 2–3 pages in per day. I write until about 2 p.m. when I go to get my kids, then I switch to Dad mode.

(Hosseini, 2012)

Science fiction writer Octavia E. Butler, Lynell George reports:

wove work around her writing windows, not the other way around . . . waking up by two, three, or four a.m., to spend time on the page–even if just to glare at it or wish for words to come–before readying herself for her pay-the-bills work. She'd plot out her plans in her journals and on wall calendars, charting not just time but also the number of pages she planned to complete (and then noting triumph when she succeeded).

(George, 2023: 110)

Creative writing involves progress, from the basics of some kind of hand and eye movement, to the inscribing, typing, etching, making of a mark that (even if done analogically on a screen, or suggested by an audio recording) represents writing's historic condition of creating a long-lasting record (if not always a permanent one). Mobility of thought and feeling as well as of the writing itself is a primary condition of creative writing.

For many of us who write creatively there is a concern simply to know whether we have moved toward any kind of completion of the work we envisaged at the start. Most often, this is something done when the imagined works are long – such as when writing a novel. But all kinds of writers have engaged in tracking and tracing their activities – not least with the aim of being better informed when setting off into future projects. While it is true works of creative writing can be given a kind of re-writing by the interpretations and critical responses they receive from general readers and professional critics alike, our creative writing is only largely mobile once – that is, at the point at which we are composing. It is in understanding those mobile moments that we learn about how creative writing happens.

References

Bauby, Jean-Dominique, *The Diving Bell and The Butterfly* (original French title *Le Scaphandre et le Papillon, 1997*), Vintage: New York, 1998.

George, Lynell, 'Patience, Practice, Perseverance, How Octavia E. Butler Became a Writer', *The American Scholar*, 92, no. 4, Autumn 2023, pp. 100–112.

Hosseini, Khaled in Noah Charney, 'Khaled Hosseini: How I Write', *Daily Beast*, July 14, 2017, https://www.thedailybeast.com/khaled-hosseini-how-i-write (Last Accessed, January 5, 2024).

Kosinski, Jerzy in Plimpton, George A. and Rocco Landesman, 'The Art of Fiction XLVI: Jerzy Kosinski', *Paris Review*, 14, no. 54, Summer 1972, pp. 183–207.

Munro, Alice, in Jeanne McCulloch and Mona Simpson, 'The Art of Fiction No. 137', *Paris Review*, 36, no. 131, Summer 1994, pp. 226–264.

Steinbeck, John, in George Plimpton and Frank Crowther, 'The Art of Fiction No. 45', *Paris Review*, 16, no. 63, Fall 1975, pp. 180–194.

8

CONNECTIONS

Joined-Up Writing

When we write creatively we make connections. Having a guiding metaphor assists us becoming aware of the nature and dimensions of those connections and, being aware, we can situate them in how we think, how we create, and how we assess what we are creating. Well-known French philosopher Paul Ricoeur (1913–2005) tells us that 'metaphor is the rhetorical process by which discourse unleashes the power that certain fictions have to rede-scribe reality' (Ricoeur, 1978: 6). It does so by connecting what Ricoeur calls 'fictions' and the reality to which they are referring. This deepens layers of meaning and, in deepening them, strengthens our understanding.

Connection-making is one of the reasons for the existence of the crea-tive arts, along with personal expression and exploration and the aspects of learning and exchange between people, between differing viewpoints, cul-tures, and circumstances.

When writing creatively, our initial connections – those connections that underpin our writerly actions – are straightforward:

Intellect and imagination. Creative writing involves the reasoning, logic, and rational functions of the human mind needed in order to make writing make sense. Because writing is designed to communicate in the absence of a speaker it must in many ways be commonsensical and recognizable. So, we clearly use our intellect when we're writing creatively, even though our understanding of creativity is that it is about the new, the original, the inventive – essentially about transcending the ordinary. We connect these two aspects of creative writ-ing, the ordinary and the extraordinary, through how we navigate our way

DOI: 10.4324/9781003174400-8

between the reasoned elements of writing and the inventive leaps of the imagination. This navigation is not one dimensional and it is not based on universal principles. How you navigate it is not the same as how I might navigate it, and that individuality is at the heart of creative writing. We can call our connections here 'bridges', meaning we actively build them and can move back and forth across them, maintaining the general comprehensibility of our writing but creating a flow between the logical, reasoning elements we use writing and the new and innovative elements we explore when doing so creatively. These connections are synapses, acting like sparks, pulses or signals, and they rely more on stimuli than on a fixed span over which we travel. At points we can be inclined to challenge ease of reading or comprehensibility because the theme or subject encourages us to do so. At other points we might be direct, unambiguous and overt. Our practice might be more immediate and random than other kinds of writing – given its heightened creativity. Finally, our intellect-imagination journey has an accentuated natural flow, so that we find associations between things along the route, while maintaining the general direction and idea of what we might say, and communicate, and explore - allowing the journey to define how the writing reads and looks and feels, – intellect and imagination agreeing, in that sense, to be guided by the motion of the journey.

Past and present. By its nature, creative writing is dependent on the past. At the most basic level, this is because in order to write we must be recording something and in recording it we are dependent on having witnessed, having thought, having been told or having felt that something. In this we are locating what has been, even if we are writing about what might be, because we draw on our established sense of context and meaning, both of which have been formed over time. While, in the spirit of creativity, our creative writing is associated with the new and original, it is also informed by traditions found in genre of writing, linguistic meaning, cultural history, depictions of logical narrative processions, and recognizable use of figures of speech. Writing is a form of communication (as well as, in the case of *creative* writing, a form of art) so it is often grounded in commonsense exchanges, where those receiving the writing are generally able to comprehend what those creating the writing are offering. In notable ways, we bond as humans through writing – and while not all cultures are literate cultures, this bonding nevertheless is globally widespread and significant. With creative writing, we therefore also bond through our shared interest in human creativity, which involves the societal influences we bring to it, our individual histories (family, friends and more) and our modes of creative expression, which are personal and cultural.

Self and others. It could be suggested that if we are only writing for ourselves then our creative writing does not involve creating associations with others. Seemingly true, if those associations with others mostly involve the public dissemination of creative writing that occurs through publishing, or the sharing of our writing with family, friends or colleagues or that activities in a creative writing workshop in a school, a community or a university. In these examples, our connecting with others through writing is common and overt. If we write something privately and show it to no one, surely that is different?

However, consider why the language you are using was forged in our human need to communicate with others. There would be no need for an exchangeable and widely recognizable language if we only had to speak to ourselves. Think too of how we came to be involved in a literate practice – that is writing – and why such literate practices exist in the society we are in. They relate to creating a sense of permanence, of recording – and while that recording, verbally, might only be for our own ears, when leaving written traces of our observations, ideas, or feelings we assume the possibility of the existence of other people (others who will read our writing). Creativity too, while able to be our version of what is new, inventive, or original relies on comparative, contextual information. It is highly likely that comparative sense comes from attempts to correlate what we have seen, felt or experienced with that depicted by others in our own and other cultures. We connect in our human world through our creative endeavors, no matter how personalized they might be. As a species our strengths are often related to our abilities to use our imaginations. This sense in which we have what we can call a 'species commitment' to creativity also strongly reflects the connections between each of us, as individuals within our species.

Those underpinning connections form the basis of our reasoning and our general perspective as creative writers. They represent core considerations about the practice of creative writing – how it works, how it forms its fundamental relationships, and about its position as an activity we humans choose to undertake and, quite frequently, have also chosen to celebrate.

Exploring the Terrain

When writing creatively, we unquestionably discover things that were not expected, along with those things we mostly did expect. We can consider these occurrences in terms of the territory through which we travel, or what we can call our writing 'terrain'.

Vistas and encounters. Vistas can be thought of as things, actions and results, along with topics and themes, ideas, and feelings that we largely expected to come across. A vista is either broad and sweeping (for example, the planned topics and theme/s of a piece of writing) or narrow but known to be ahead of you, a projection (in simple terms), such as the next scene in a screenplay or the planned ending of a novel. An encounter, however, is something or someone you come upon unexpectedly, a discovery by chance. At times an encounter presents challenges. It can throw you off balance, so that you need to prop and consider what it is, and why, and what to do with it or about it or in light of it. Creative writers are not unique in having to deal with both the expected and the unexpected. However, there is a distinctiveness about what occurs in creative writing because our reaction to it is likely to be etched (perhaps literally) into a record of how we reacted. An encounter in creative writing can be your recognition that the character you thought would be central to the viewpoint of your story does not interest you, and you far prefer the viewpoint of one of the (previously) minor characters. An encounter can be the discovery of a piece of information, a new contemporary or historical fact that changes the sequence of scenes planned in your screenplay. An encounter can be the reading of a poem on a different main theme or subject to the one you are writing, but whose form is attractive to you, and so you adopt it.

As creative writers, we experience things in creative writing unfolding as vistas and as encounters. This is both in the content of what we write and in the technical aspects of our writing. The fluidity of our imaginations heightens the dynamism of this relationship. Even in the most planned of writing projects we are venturing through vistas and encounters. How we respond to these determines much about our success – we are looking ahead, in a forward-facing vista-like vision; while, simultaneously we are aware of the potential for encounters on our journey. This is one of the reasons creative writing cannot be thought of as a series of linear steps, one occurring after the other (sometimes described as 'stages' and labeled 'pre-writing', 'writing' and 'post-writing' (Harper, 2019: 64–77). In fact, we are fluidly venturing all the time, with a wider view of where we are heading, but with the likelihood of encounters that alter our approach, or reinforce our sense of direction, or introduce new ideas or stimulate our imagination, or result in the beginning of a new project altogether.

Constructions. Writing relies on constructing. We regularly hear writers talking about this – about 'constructing a story', about the 'construction of a scene', about 'structuring'. The frequency of this commentary is the result of our active role in making something. When artificial intelligence (AI) began to be used for writing projects, one of the first challenges was around how active or passive we humans were in the creation of a piece of writing. Did it matter that a human being might not have generated the first iteration of a poem or a story? What if they didn't create that, but they used AI iteration as something to build upon, to mold and change according to their own preferences – was that okay, or did the AI create the poem or story?

Our belief in the connections made by our active constructing relates to a human belief in our interactive role with the world at large. Whether we always see this role as positive is perhaps another consideration; however, the underlying idea that we are not passive participants in the world or in our own lives is strong. As creative writers we embody and exemplify such a constructionist outlook – after all, as creative writers we are by definition makers, we are creators. In that vein, how we work is artful, most often intentional; what we do has a style and a pattern; we lay things out in forms and we have methods of working and imagine the ways in which the readers or audiences for our work might potentially engage with it. With these things in mind, 'design' is a useful concept for what we do, design as that concept is also used by architects. Poet, novelist, and short story writer Lorraine Lopez sees it this way in her chapter 'The Architecture of Story' (Lopez, 2013: 9). She also talks about 'blueprints', 'building materials', and 'pouring the foundation'. In Lopez's description constructions are shared between the builder of them and those - the reader, the audience - who live in what is built. Lopez writes:

> Stories, while inspired by dreams, are the products of an intentional process of many steps – from blueprinting to final touch up – and like houses, well-constructed stories invite readers to live and breathe within their walls, traveling from room to room, or scene to scene, as they inhabit and experience, along with the characters, their distinctive architecture.
>
> *(Lopez, 2013: 9)*

This description reminds us of the ways in which shared experience (or, more accurately, the expectation of shared experiences) lies at the heart of creative writing.

Associations. 'Associative realizations' – to coin a definition – are destinations (that is, somewhere visited) that are part of our creative writing mapping. We move through our undertaking of creative writing with things in mind – themes, subjects, stories, images, ideas – and the associative outcomes we create are fluid. The action of bringing things into play, bringing them together, is an associative practice, and our final maps of what we gain from a project, and what readers or audiences might gain from a project are changed because of this. In Psychology, 'associative' is used to describe the relationship between actions and results. This works as a way of navigating creative writing too. We both actively create associations and we are moved to action by the associations we create. The realization of something or someone having a relationship with something or someone else (literally and/or figuratively) is a stimulus to thought and feeling, and while we certainly might bring this pre-formed to a writing project, we also form it as we write. It is a product of the interaction of our vision and of our understanding.

Finally, we might consider how we navigate creative writing when we find ourselves experiencing both triumphs and challenges. The response we have when we learn something in our writing works, or something doesn't work can guide our future action. This kind of associative learning has been studied for generations, and continues to inform the thinking of psychologists. This 1997 summary by Edward Wasserman and Ralph Miller continues to be relevant:

> Although no longer dominant in experimental psychology, associative learning remains a highly active area of research and theory. Work here still focuses on the behavior of animals, but the study of associative learning in human beings is growing in interest and importance (Shanks, 1994). Most noteworthy is recent research in causal perception and the success that has been achieved there by associative theories (Allan, 1993; Young, 1995). Researchers in neuroscience and cognitive science have also become interested in associative learning.
>
> *(Wasserman and Miller, 1997: 575)*

As Wasserman and Miller point out 'the laws of associative learning are complex, and many modern theorists posit the involvement of attention, memory, and information processing in such basic conditioning phenomena as overshadowing and blocking, and the effects of stimulus preexposure on later conditioning' (Wasserman and Miller, 1997: 573). It is the 'conditioning phenomena' that is of primary interest to us here, when we consider what occurs when we write creatively. We know memory, attention, and information processing are involved in creative writing; but, we also know that creative writing entails decision-making that is multi-dimensional.

Some of our creative decisions – which are structured by the nature of writing – will result in desired results, some will not. Some will please us but, if we are seeking communication with others, not necessarily please a reader or an audience. We each learn to write and read mostly for pragmatic reasons; that is, basic communication in our literate cultures, essential understanding of the world and activities around us when we live in those cultures.

We learn to write creatively because we want to express ourselves, or explore our individual and/or cultural identity, or enhance our self-awareness. Or because we are moved by a cultural tradition involving writing or wish to record a moment of history, or to examine such a tradition or to tell a story to others, or to reflect on something beautiful, or tremendous, monumental, close, possible, or improbable, to illustrate an emotion or somehow caption a moment, or to provoke a thought or to experiment with written language or . . . This list is far from exhaustive.

We are not born with the ability to write. When taught to write we are not sanctioned first and foremost to write creatively. While we might culturally revere literary works, we practically need a population that can communicate commonsensically and professional communities that can share knowledge in their fields. The ability to write creatively, while fundamental to many creative industries (publishing, media, performance industries, and so on) is for the majority of people a supplement to the ability to communicate plainly or in their specialized field. With that in mind, then, education generally does not prioritize teaching solutions to creative writing problems. Simply put, one aspect of association we can need to unlearn are those behaviors that encourage us to avoid writing problems. Instead, as creative writers we are required to see associative learning as part of the active experience in which we engage, to view writing problems as productive challenges. While naïve to say we might celebrate rather than lament a difficult writing situation, a change of perspective to see the associative learning we gain from creative writing failures as something we can embrace could well be empowering.

The things we experience in our creative writing, and the techniques we use to respond or relate to them, map our progress from starting somewhere to heading somewhere. Not all creative writers see that starting point the same way (some might say it was when they first thought of an idea for a piece of creative writing, or when they first had an experience that they now plan to write about; others might say that they start to write when they physically begin to put down 'on paper' the elements of their poem or script of story). Similarly, where creative writing arrives is not universally viewed the same way. Certainly, many creative writers view the completion of a project to be when the piece of writing is itself at a conclusion – the final page, the final line, the final word. But other writers focus on the experience of the writing and the conclusion of a project – the arrival point – is therefore the point at which the experience seems complete. This is one of the reasons why we hear writerly echoes of 'a project is never completed only abandoned' (to paraphrase a comment most often attributed to French poet Paul Valéry (1871–1945) and related to the earlier 'Art is never finished, only abandoned', attributed to Renaissance polymath Leonardo da Vinci (1452–1519).

This abandonment might not relate to (or only to) the physical object that is created, and whether it is in some way considered complete, good, ideal, appropriate, satisfying. It could relate to the emotions we find inherent in our practice and the feelings we have about that creative writing practice and the holistic nature of the association we make between us writing creatively and the results of us doing this.

References

Harper, Graeme, *Critical Approaches to Creative Writing*, Abington: Routledge, 2019.
Lopez, Lorraine, 'The Architecture of Story', in *A Companion to Creative Writing*, Graeme Harper (ed), Oxford: Blackwell, 2013, pp. 9–23.
Ricoeur, Paul, *The Rule of Metaphor*, London: Routledge & Kegan Paul, 1978.
Wasserman, Edward and Ralph Miller, 'Elementary Associative Learning', *Annual Review of Psychology*, 48, 1997, pp. 573–607.

9

CREATIVE WRITING CHOICES

Routes

Choice is both a desired human condition and a demanding one. Deciding on a route toward or away from something is one of those choices. A route is a direction and a way ('way' meaning a method as well as a path or track). A way can refer to our application of skills, and it can refer to states of mind, perspectives, and sentiments. The routes we take through our creative writing are direct or indirect. When writing we are commonly intending to make progress toward some kind of conclusion – that is, to a point where we feel there is nothing more to add, for now. Any kind of progress in writing involves routes taken or not taken.

We don't all start writing creatively at the same time (in the day or night, or in life, for that matter). We don't all write the same way. We don't all write with the same outcomes in mind. We don't all make the same decisions about what to write and why we write. To state the obvious, we each begin somewhere, determined by who we are, and by our personal and social circumstances. We head toward some kind of end point, determined by us, by the circumstances and influences of our lives, by creative choices, by suggestions from others (if we show our things to anyone along the way), and by fortuitous influences along the way. In essence, we make, or we find routes, and we take them.

DOI: 10.4324/9781003174400-9

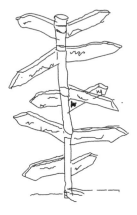

The Robert Frost poem "The Road Not Taken" is very likely the best-known poetic musing in the English-speaking world on decision-making and route taking. It begins:

> Two roads diverged in a yellow wood,
> And sorry I could not travel both
> And be one traveler, long I stood
> And looked down one as far as I could
> To where it bent in the undergrowth.
>   (Frost, 1950: 556)

Frost goes on to explore the dimensions of choice and the influence of impulse. Though the poem has found a readership as a deep rumination, its playfulness is one of its main strengths. We read it as much for its mischievous rhymes as for its pensive musing. This playfulness also reminds us, if we dig a little deeper, that Frost wrote this poem as a joke for his friend, the Welsh poet Edward Thomas, whose trouble deciding on which route to take when he and Frost were out walking together was one of the motivations behind Frost writing the poem. Other interpretations are also well-known, including this highlighted by Jennifer Bouchard:

> Frost also explained another inspiration for this poem at the 1953 Bread Loaf Writer's Conference. He said that he was thinking about a friend of his who had gone off to war and always regretted not choosing the other road. The real internal conflict for his friend, though, was that he knew if

he did choose the other road, he would have been sorry he did not go off
to help in World War I.

(Bouchard, 2014: 166)

Frost often wrote to Thomas about the war, and the sense of routes taken or
not taken was common in those letters. For example, in this letter from Frost
to Thomas on November 6, 1916:

> And yet you know how I feel about the war. I have stopped asseverating
> from a sense of fitness. You rather shut me up by enlisting. Talk is almost
> too cheap when all your friends are facing bullets. I don't believe I ought
> to enlist (since I am of course an American), but if I can't enlist, at least I
> refuse to talk sympathy beyond a certain point. I did set myself to wish this
> country into the war. I made a little noise on the subject, but soon found
> I wasn't half as good at the noise as some who cared less. (Has Harold
> Begbie enlisted?) When all the world is facing danger, it's a shame not to be
> facing danger for any reason, old age, sickness, or any other. Words won't
> make the shame less. There's no use trying to make out that the shame we
> suffer makes up for the more heroic things we don't suffer. No more of this
> for a long time. Are not the magazines chuckfull of it?

(Frost, 2014: 503)

'The Road Not Taken' is a poem with layers of intention and meaning – for the
reader, of course, but also clearly for the writer. We know the story behind the
poem, so we can get some insight into those writerly intentions and meanings.

It is possible to choose our writing routes for more than one reason, and
to have more than one motivation for continuing to follow a particular path.
It is also possible, as Frost's conclusion tells us, that we write with a sense of
simultaneity. That is, while we are following one technical route of inscribing
our thoughts and feeling (because writing is inscribing so we can't overlay
different bits of it without it becoming illegible) we are also following more
than one imaginative, emotional, or cerebral route. From this perspective, our
choice of what to write down (or inscribe) is a singular choice, but we are
aware of other things on our journey that we are not writing.

While Thomas had written prose and reviews, he didn't publish his first
poem until late 1914. Composing all his poetry in the three years between
1914 and 1917, he was killed by an artillery shell on April 9, 1917 in
Pas-de-Calais, France. Frost wrote his first poem, 'My Butterfly: An Elegy'
in 1894, when he was 18 years old, and his final poem, 'In the Clearing',
in 1962, 66 years later. He died in January 1963 at the age of 88, following complications from prostate surgery. A great many of Thomas's poems

were published posthumously. Frost, on the other hand, published poetry relatively consistently throughout his life, though he struggled for early success, eventually moving to England in search of more publisher interest in his poems. That move paid off. He published his first collection *A Boy's Will* (Nutt) in 1913 and his second *North of Boston* (Nutt) in 1914, returning to the USA in 1915 after the breakout of World War I, substantially more successful than when he had left.

Such biographical stories as those of Frost and Thomas provide us with another example of routes taken. The relationships between our lives and our creative writing are complex, and they are entwined – not simply for the obvious reason that physical and mental experiences influence us, but because the imagination and human communication are particularly open to shaping. What appears as technical writerly decisions, decisions some might refer to as decisions of writer's craft, are underpinned and influenced by our lives well beyond those decisions. Robert Frost's poem encourages thinking on this. His conclusion, if it is a conclusion, is that choice has many dimensions. So much so, in fact, that our impulse to go one way or another, choose one thing or another, carries equal possibility of success and equal likelihood of disappointment. The last two lines of the poem leave open the thought that no choice is entirely good; and evoke the idea, notionally if not practically, that going both directions simultaneously would have been the better result:

I took the one less traveled by,
And that has made all the difference.
                    (Frost, 1950: 557)

In all cases, pragmatically (if not in terms of our range of thoughts and extent of feelings), the technical demands of writing mean that we have to choose. Clearly, when we write something it fills the space that could have been occupied by other writing. While you can overlay a word on another, and then on another, and so on and so on, the effect, of course, is to eventually obscure everything that is written. We choose to occupy space with some words, some stories, some ideas, some images, some interpretations, some scenes, some summaries, some words, and not others . . . to leave other things out, even if we are still thinking or feeling those things.

Such a graphic occupation determines what we see or hear (both as writers and readers/audiences), and even as writing technologies have changed over time our ability to subvert this basic physical fact is limited. Creative writing, offering more extensive expressive choice, makes the choices even more challenging, because the points of reference are greater and the available routes more numerous.

Purpose and Perception

Our choice of routes through a creative writing project is based on **purpose** and **perception**. These are not separate entities they are interwoven, and they too are associative. They are associative because the imagination in order to write requires the intellect (to assist with structure and form and communication), and the intellect in order to be creative requires the imagination (to assist with invention, and originality, and novelty). Pointing to these aspects, individually, assists in considering all the potential elements of interweaving that are going on when we write creatively. We can select categories of action, reaction, interpretation, and understanding and consider them under either the rubric of **purpose** or that of **perception**. In either case, we discover signposts, and directions we might take.

The possible **purpose** behind a route we introduce and/or follow in creative writing can relate to any number of things. Purpose here refers to a logical, analytical choice we have made to follow a particular route. Here is a selection of considerations related to purpose:

- **Effect.** Either a way of composing or a direction in the content, theme, subject, that is reasoned will produce a certain kind of communicative or aesthetic effect. That is, be likely to initiate a chosen kind of response.
- **Point made.** A decision made that whatever point we wished to make – and 'point' here viewed broadly as inclusion of an idea, an observation, a reference to an emotion – has been made.
- **Additions.** That more is needed to complete a scene, a contemplation, more to be said or explored, outlined, revealed, considered . . . A route taken can be seeking to add something.
- **Clarifications.** That something is still unclear.
- **Asides.** That pace or subject, character, emotional context . . . that there is a benefit from offering an aside, in support, in contrast, on which something might be built later in the story, the script, the poem.
- **Adding depth.** Too shallow, presently, we take a route anticipated to deepen part of a project or the entire project. Not dispersing ideas, observations, or feelings, but delving further into them.
- **Associations (the particular and the general).** Reasoned connections between things and experiences. Routes in how we write creatively are often a reasoned collection of associations. That is not to say they are not also felt – and we'll see below how reasoning and sensing are never entirely dissociated in creative writing.
- **Summing up.** Recently in a writing project, a Series Editor at a well-known academic press suggested every author in an upcoming edited collection include a 'summing up' at the conclusion of each section of their chapters.

For some authors this felt unnecessary, for others it provided an opportunity for their own clarification. The suggested amendment was neither absolutely right nor absolutely wrong – as a compositional route it represented an opinion about the providing of information, explanation, clarity, connectiveness, perhaps (some might say) even duty of care to the reader. In creative writing we choose to sum up, sometimes, to make a route more clear – for ourselves, as the writer, and for others, as readers or audience. We might consider this a point of pause or as a form of resonance.

– **Speculation.** The reasons behind taking a particular route in a writing project can indeed be speculative. Such a suggestion is not to shirk responsibility for making a choice – because we can remind ourselves that creative writing is writing with heightened imagination. People seek out works of creative writing not solely because they move along logically, methodically or commonsensically. One of the joys of creative writing is the conjectures, the interpretations, perhaps the suppositions, and the fantasies. Knowledge and understanding when we write creatively are less dependent on following traditions laid out in disciplines of scientific, social, or cultural analyses. Even though many writers – poets, novelists, screenwriters, and others – draw on established knowledge in various fields of human endeavor, and often attempt to be factually correct, the individual nature of what creative writers do provides opportunities for speculation. We certainly learn by writing creatively, and we learn from reading works of creative writing, but the learning is grounded in independence and a greater degree of self-reliance than we find in many other realms of human knowledge.

The possible **perception** behind a route we introduce and/or follow in creative writing can relate to any number of things. Perception here referring to our feelings our emotions, connected with the choices we make. Here is a selection of considerations related to perception:

– **Rhythmic.** We feel it as much as see or hear the rhythm, the pace, the tempo of a piece of writing. In this sense we could say that a piece of creative writing has a kind of pulse, and we choose to maintain or change that pulse along the way – that is the rhythmic beat of a piece of work.
– **Sequence-making.** Our approach to a project includes notions of *what* happens *when*, not necessarily in terms of structural things like plot in a story; but, rather in terms of the content of a piece of writing, no matter what kind of writing it is, and our method of writing it. Anecdotally, we hear creative writers discussing how they 'wrote the ending first' or 'revised a lot'. These are statements about sequence. We can, or course, reason why a set of things should appear in a poem or story of script in a certain order – but in creative writing sequences are more sensed than they are methodized. This is why creative writers play with notions of time and

place, use analepsis (flashback) and prolepsis (flashforward), deepen their explorations with metaphor and analogy, change viewpoints, overlay sensory information (sights, sounds). Sequence is sensory in creative writing, we seek out a holistic experience.

- **Echoic**. Resonance not only creates rhythm in writing it relates to moods, tones, and reflections. This echoic sense of creative writing we can think of as conveying a thought or feeling so that it is memorable – in other words, the repeating of something is a starting point for remembering. However, repetition is no guarantee of a response, so what we are referring to in creative writing is resonance – meaning more than simple repetition; rather, enriched or enhanced return of ideas or emotions (and we see this in all genre of creative writing – echoic senses of subjects and themes, observations and ideas).
- **Reflective**. Our senses work by detection. We detect the texture of something, by touching it; we detect a sound, a voice, music, and its volume and its timbre and its pitch and make assumptions about meaning and intention. Color sends messages to us in a similar way – red, blue, green, pink, purple – every color is interpreted by our brain and this influences behavior and emotions. As does light – its intensity, its color, its direction. In creative writing, reflection combines this kind of sensory work we naturally undertake when we're in the world with the analytical we have in mind when writing – we draw on our natural mode of using our senses to interpret, and when we choose to reflect in writing we use linguistic tools to embody that detection, the things we have sensed and are analyzing.
- **Informational**. The routes we choose through a writing project might contain points where we provide – in narrative terms – exposition (that is, background or explanation). This inclusion of exposition relates to conveying meaning and purpose – and through our creative writing we sense this for ourselves as much as we seek to convey it to others. Route-making based on the provision of information seems, in some way, mundane in a mode of communication (that is, writing) that is also an art form (that is, creative writing). And yet, in whatever form it takes – in poetry, in prose, in the script for a computer game – we create points at which information is offered, and often then built upon.
- **Questioning**. We are interested as much in what we are trying to discover as we are in what we are trying to convey in our creative writing. It is a common theme in writer's biographies, this seeking to discover through writing. From playwright, Edward Albee: 'All of a sudden I discover that I have been thinking about a play. This is usually between six months and a year before I actually sit down and start typing it out' (Albee, 1963: 60). From novelist E. L. Doctorow: 'You write to find out what it is that you're writing' (Doctorow, 1981: B1). From short story writer and essayist, Flannery O'Connor: 'I don't have my novel outlined and I have to write to

discover what I am doing. Like the old lady, I don't know so well what I think until I see what I say; then I have to say it over again' (O'Connor, 1979: 5).

Solutions

Often the choices we make will create discernible patterns in how we go about our writing. These can be patterns of composition that occur over more than one project, and knowing how we create these patterns, and how we might vary our approaches, and what effect happens when we choose one aspect or another to move us along through a project – all this generates usable knowledge to get us from the start of a project to the finish.

Like any skill, we work our way toward a solution, which validates an approach, and then we consider one of our skills to be drawing on that approach we have tried and applied. In this sense, we can find our destinations across a range of creative writing projects will be similar – when it comes to solutions to technical writing problems or even to how we manage imaginative leaps. But we also find new paths, establish new solutions – and in doing so create new means of traveling through a project, generating points we reach along the way – in our work, and in doing our work. The symbiotic relationship between the work produced – the physical piece of writing you make – and the writing itself is particularly poignant in creative writing because the practice and the end results reflect the fluidity of the activity, the conversation between thought and sentiments, ourselves as writers and the others who might receive our works.

References

Albee, Edward in Digby Diehl, 'Edward Albee: An Interview', *The Transatlantic Review*, no. 13, 48. Summer 1963, pp. 57–72.

Bouchard, Jennifer, *Introduction to Literary Context: American Poetry of the 20th Century*, Hackensack, NJ: Salem Press, 2014.

Doctorow, E.L., in Randi Henderson, '"Ragtime" to Riches: Non-writing Is Doctorow's Neurosis', *The Baltimore Sun*, March 31, 1981, pp. 57–72.

Frost, Robert, *A Boy's Will*, London: Nutt, 1913.

Frost, Robert, *The Letters of Robert Frost*, Donald Sheehy, Mark Richardson and Robert Faggen (eds), Cambridge: Belknap Press, 2014.

Frost, Robert, *North of Boston*, London: Nutt, 1914.

Frost, Robert, 'The Road Not Taken', in *The Oxford Book of American Verse*, F. O. Mathieson (ed), Oxford: Oxford University Press, 1950. Originally published 1915.

O'Connor, Flannery, *The Habit of Being: Letters of Flannery O'Connor*, Sally Fitzgerald (ed), New York: Farrar, Straus and Giroux, 1979.

10
ARRIVING

In creative writing, as with all things, knowing you have arrived is relatively straightforward if you knew where you were going in the first place; and, if you can clearly recognize the place you are now, based on those original plans. Of course, that is if on the way you didn't change your mind about where you were going, and have headed to this new location instead. Also, if while traveling you personally did not change. In the latter cases, where you have arrived might not be where you had planned to be going or now be where you have ended up.

We commonly want to go where we choose to go, and any disruption or forced deviation from that is greeted with concern or exasperation. Sometimes we regulate our communal human movements, in the name of safety or secrecy, ownership or value (the beachfront property with 'Private Access' to the beach is a declaration of both these things). Individually, however, our expectations are often counter to this – we expect to be able to go where we want, and when we want. Consider for a moment all those stories, real and conceived, that center on the relocating of someone against their will – whether the stories of imprisonment, stories of removal, or stories of cultural denigration. Consider, too, the simple actions of traveling to work somewhere beyond home, and the sense in which your 'commute' (a specific, linguistically defined experience, as it were) has length and difficulty and character and degrees of consistency. The sardonic fact we all face, as creative writers have explored as much if not more than Existentialist philosophers, is that by being born our 'destination' is ultimately one place, and that is death. Our beginning is also ultimately our end. It is a defining factor that determines the *extent* of our human narrative, but not its shape or style, not all of its conditions of travel nor its depth of meaning.

DOI: 10.4324/9781003174400-10

Ours is a narrative of direction – but that direction might not be geographic, or involve any shift of location; rather, it can be a journey of internal discovery, an expansion of knowledge, the creating of relationships with others, the pursuit of arriving at a point of satisfaction that bears no resemblance to the physical exertions of mountain climbers or lunar astronauts, but some of the intentional strength that impels both of these.

By and large, human beings move, and that movement can be external and/or internal, physical and/or mental, intellectual and/or emotional, or any combination of these factors, in varying degrees of strength and weakness, resilience and rigidity, so that our direction is simultaneously defined and open to our interpretation, adjustment, consideration, and our determination – a place, in some fashion; an attitude, in another fashion.

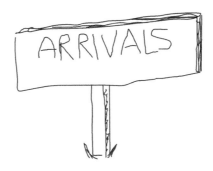

In creative writing we arrive because of many factors, and with the employment and influence of many modes of movement – even if these modes are not of physical journeying but, rather, of thinking, imagining, and engaging with what is around us or considering what we have invented in our imaginations.

Our arrival in creative writing is, therefore, determined by our own perception of where we are going, and why we are going there, and what we expect to see (that is, create) when we have arrived. Some might argue that if we take the arts to refer to activities of the creative industries, as many of the commercial arts practices tend to be, then a considerable number of artists (including writers) are required to produce work that heads to destinations predetermined by people other than themselves. This is most often the case in those creative industries sub-sectors where the end results relate to the industrial rather than craft economy end results (in other words, in those creative industries where full-time commercial teams work to produce arts products and experiences rather than where independent creative practitioners work toward their own creative results; for example, the leisure software industry or a commercial pottery, versus the individual painter or freelance musician). Those analyzing the creative industries have sometimes struggled to apply the same set of principles and notions to the extent and volume of these different activities involving humans creatively making and doing things – that is, industrially or in the numerous types of individual craft practice. In actuality, even when the arts are commercial they are grounded in and informed by the application of the individual human imagination for connection-making, communication, and celebration of how we humans think and feel.

For creative writers, a work might certainly be written to order, or pre-determined by some external force – such things as a strictly contracted word length from a publisher or the demands of matching a popular genre format or the needs of a wider production team in a media company, or a commissioned style for a song or computer game. And yet, regardless of how much we think of our readers or audiences, much of the attraction of engaging in creative writing comes from a relative freedom to determine how we proceed and where we end up. This personal creative autonomy has attracted a number of us to creative writing (I certainly include myself as one of those attracted by it). It is in some way a declaration of pushing back against our 'ultimate' fateful human destination by taking charge, and creating, and exploring, and exchanging with others, and celebrating, and appreciating, and making some kind of minor contribution to the experience of living, for ourselves and perhaps for others.

Of course, we shouldn't generalize. Those who enjoy writing creatively are as varied as any other group of people. Additionally what we humans do in the world only partly contributes to who we are. And yet, creative writers do appear to have some common traits and having a sense of a destination, an arrival point, is one of them (to complete a poem; to capture a thought; to relate an idea; to write an historical novel; to explore a feeling; to 'get something out'; to share with your children; to win a writing competition; to see the film your wrote produced and screened; to know how the story you have in mind ends; to closely consider something you see every day; to make sense of a thought; to live an alternative week or year in some imagined alternative guise; to put down on paper what seems impossible to grasp; to ponder in print).

We are always using our compass with individual intent, and often with a capacity for change, evolution of our reasoning, impressions and intentions. We're heading somewhere, perhaps hoping that we will not lose the energy, or the time, or the motivation to reach that place. And we're engaging in a practice that we know involves both art and communication – that can in varying degrees stretch or alter language for artistic effect, while attempting to deliver in written words pleasure, insight, observation, prediction, recollection. Our compass certainly has its work cut out for it.

Creative writing is not a purely pragmatic pursuit. Nor is it always idealistic. It is not routinely like any other writing. Nor does it consistently involve making written language strange. It is one of the misnomers about creativity that is continually the quirky, idiosyncratic or outlandish. In fact, it can also be conventional, innovative (meaning positively new), transcendent, and valuable. It can be incisive and direct. It is regularly productive and it is oftentimes worthwhile. Mark Runco and Garrett Jaeger, in a short exploratory 'Correction' in the *Creativity Research Journal*, entitled 'The Standard Definition of Creativity', alert readers to this when they say:

> Originality is vital for creativity but is not sufficient. Ideas and products that are merely original might very well be useless. They may be unique or uncommon for good reason! Originality can be found in the word salad of a psychotic and can be produced by monkeys on word processors. A truly random process will often generate something that is merely original. So again, originality is not alone sufficient for creativity. Original things must be effective to be creative. Like originality, effectiveness takes various forms. It may take the form of (and be labeled as) usefulness, fit, or appropriateness.
> Effectiveness may take the form of value.
>
> *(Runco and Jaeger, 2012: 92)*

Runco and Jaeger's 'appropriateness', 'value', and 'effectiveness' are accessible and attainable measures - for everyone. In other words, while it is true that creativity embodies the metaphysical, the intangible, and the abstract, it is also approachable. Strategies of action can be created and methods developed. This is not to oversimplify what creative writers do or to reduce this to a list of 'how to' exercises or to procedures that merely need to be replicated in order to be successful at creative writing. Rather, it is propose that appropriateness, value and effectiveness can be evaluated and, with a destination in mind, that they can be determined - for every piece of creative writing.

Our arrival at our destination in creative writing can involve any or all of the following:

- **Completed works.** When we see the creative writing we have undertaken represented by works we consider complete – even if we mean by 'complete' something along the lines of 'as much as I can do or want to do' – we have in effect arrived. Like any place of arrival, our location will be anywhere from spectacularly good to disappointingly inadequate (and any point in between). We cannot assume our arrival in creative writing is the point at which the work in front of us is perfect (in our eyes or anyone else's) any more than we can assume anything else in our lives is perfect. That arrival is the physical representation of the work we have been doing - one piece of creative writing, or many - that we consider now to be done. These completed works can be the primary aspect of our arrival, and many times they are.

– **Your experiences**. Creative writing is experiences, any number of actions that happen over varying lengths of time and for a variety of reasons – both initiated by you, the writer, and initiated by circumstances around you (demands to do other things; alternative ways of expressing yourself; changes of place, cultural and social and economic conditions that have a macro impact, and into which you are drawn). It could be that we arrive in creative writing simply by doing it – that it is the actions of it that are our destination, our undertaking of it. While this idea is not extraordinary or out of keeping with how we commonly view human experiences, consider how often we are encouraged to associate creative writing first and foremost with the things made, not with the making. And yet, for you the physiological and psychological experiences of the making could be paramount. Which is not to say you don't value the works you produce. But maybe you arrive in your creative writing by being an active creative writer – regardless of whether you ever complete anything, or whether such completed work is ever offered to others.

– **Evidence of having written**. So much changed in literary culture when, in the latter decades of the 20th century, the world evolved from the predigital to the modern digital. Computer scientists appeared to notice what might occur before writers did – and the early days of the home computer immediately brought technologists' concerns about what would be lost from the record of literary culture. It went beyond this too, as those who were helping bring about the modern digital revolution also showed themselves to be aware of how many things we humans do leave behind a physical trail of that doing. We can think back to comments from those in libraries and in museums, who also began to wonder what role they might play in preserving evidence of our writing. Here from 2000:

> More and more, people are reading directly from computer screens—particularly when viewing materials that were designed for computer display, such as web pages. The best computers displays are still quite expensive, but every year they get cheaper and better. It will be a long time before computers match the convenience of books for general reading . . .
>
> *(Arms, 2000: 11)*

Undoubtedly, much did change and whereas prior to the home computer writers could track their writing in paper drafts and scribbled changes, soon the record of having written was contained in a far narrower collection of digital 'documents'. Frequently it was erased altogether, as creative writers wrote over their previous drafts.

But our arrival point did not change as much as envisaged. While certainly the paper evidence decreased in frequency and volume, the record of our writing grew and has grown since in other ways. The traffic of conversation in emails and texts arguably exceeds that which occurred in letters to friends or colleagues in the pre-digital era. The record of earlier drafts, while often erased by later drafts, remains as what we can call a 'trace in our minds', recorded not today in the paper file sitting on our desk but in the changes in compositional strategies that make changing something in a creative writing draft so much simpler and quicker. In addition, by the early 21st century, the proliferation of types of artificial intelligence and through them an increased ability to mine data from the World Wide Web, has meant that digitized records are available are also more discoverable.

Evidence of our creative writing has been, and always will be, more than the final works we produce. This additional evidence is significant in our sense of writing because it represents the spectrum of things that occur when we write. We arrive at creative writing not only by doing it, but by leaving behind (in our memories and in our physical environments) such traces. These traces of our writing represent purpose and play, intention and exploration, the evolution of ideas and feelings that make creative writing a widely chosen human activity – a record of the interactions we each have before, during, and after our writing. Whether in our memories or there on the desk in front of us, such evidence contributes to the creation of writerly habitats.

We should not ignore the importance of what might be considered the auxiliary evidence of our creative writing in our sense of having reached a destination. To risk laboring the metaphor, we navigate to our places of writing and can have definite senses of where we write and in what ways we best support our writing (particular desks, chairs, places in a room, rooms in a house, ways we set up our tables and bookshelves, things pinned to walls, silence, music playing, degrees of heat or cool . . ., and so on). Evidence of our writing is manifest by us, and even if much of the paper associated with this has disappeared in the digital age we identify as writers by how we occupy time and space, and we leave evidence of that occupation, and the ways in which we interact with the world.

- **Reasons and intentions**. We arrive at conclusions about our reasons for writing creatively and pursue our intentions for doing it (changeable though they might be). We can consider one point of arrival to be our fathoming out (more or less) what those reasons and intentions happen to be. It could be that fathoming represents a point of personal revelation and identity-making that has otherwise been absent. Our reasons and intentions also can be devoid of the pragmatic concerns of making a living – because, and not to overemphasize this but merely to reiterate, most people who write creatively do not live off the results of their writing – or it might be they represent an artistic side we have not otherwise acknowledged; or they could feature life stories and experiences that we realize are deserving of recording; or a reason might unearth a bond with others in our lives we hadn't realized existed; and intention can alert us to an element of our thinking of philosophy or emotional make-up that we had not previously considered. Creative writing traverses our reasoning side and our imaginative side (broadly speaking, reflective of the left-brain/right-brain configuration suggested by those who argue for a theory of differing human brain hemispheres). Even if considering such theory more myth than reality, we can see that creative writing has to navigate between the commonsense communication that must inform writing (where we have to make sense when we are not there to interpret our inscribed communication for other people) and the most inventive use of language and exploration of ideas and feelings that might inform a creative project. The reasons and intentions for choosing to do this are, in themselves, a destination – not everyone chooses to travel this route (again, to work with our metaphor): why did you choose to do so?

- **Types of satisfaction**. Being satisfied with completing a project is not the same satisfaction we gain from exchanging our finished project with others. If we desire both results, we also have to take on modes of disseminating our work, and come to some conclusions about what we consider satisfactory results. For example, there are creative writers who would deem the completion of a short story or a poem they consider their best to be a result beyond any other satisfaction. There are other creative writers who would not feel satisfied unless that work was submitted to, accepted by, and published by an independent arbiter. The former could be considered a personal aesthetic or emotional choice, the latter a more communal or professional choice. Both are forms of satisfaction. There are some of us who would not be satisfied unless those we love enjoy reading what we have written. There are others of us who would like most to achieve commercial success, or to see something we have written alert someone to a social, cultural, or personal issue. Satisfaction can be most achieved by some creative writers when they have collaborated with others – perhaps colleagues, friends, or students – and completed work together. Others don't feel a need for completion of any work at all, but find most satisfaction in an experience during writing where they have found out something new, or written a particularly good line, or chosen the perfect word or read something out to the laughter of friends or caught the right tone, or simply confirmed, for themselves, that an observation was worthy of recording.
- **Moving on**. For those for whom creative writing is mostly a joy (even when a labor) our destination, our arrival could also be our setting off again. Arriving can be confirmation of the ability to undertake creative writing, and so we start one project (or more than one) and continue on,

feeling (more or less) that we have learnt something. We may have learnt a new technique we now wish to explore more extensively or touched on a topic we didn't have opportunity (or reason) to consider in our previous writing session but now want to do in a new one. Creative writing can be momentary for some people – in that they complete one project, or a small number of projects, but then no others. Or it can be a lifelong activity. We might not know which it is for us when we first start writing – but if we do find one project becomes part of a continuum then moving forward is, in that sense, a point of arrival. For many of us stopping is then unthinkable. This is creative writing as transience or unsettleness. rather than creative writing as project-bound. Interestingly, literary theory has explored this. Theoreticians have considered readers as authors, reading and re-reading works with different personal, cultural, and historical contexts around them initiating alternate views of what the writing might mean or explore or represent. Creative writers have likewise been renewed, over and over again in their continued writing.

'This kind of light we would like to shed on the place of human arrival . . .', say Gert Hofmann and Snježana Zorić in *Topodynamics of Arrival: Essays on Self and Pilgrimage* (2012),

> . . . [is the] light of philosophical and spiritual awareness that includes the twilight of poetic ambivalence and existential doubt, light that unveils the ambivalent and perhaps transcending nature of the place itself, its inspirational dynamic and imaginative motility more than its functional position within the coordinates of established sociocultural systems.
>
> *(Hofman and Zorić, 2012: 12)*

Here the 'place' is a location, one in which there is 'awareness' and a 'dynamic' and 'motility'. This is a productive way to think of where our creative writing compass might take us, and how we will respond to that arrival.

There is no required arrival time or place for most creative writers, and much that we do is defined by our autonomy of practice. We can choose to decide (or have decided for us) a particular destination. We can head toward something with a definite sense or have only a vague notion of where we might end up. We can celebrate changes in direction and alterations in route and side journeys that find us generating new projects or alternative projects or notes for future creative explorations. Or we might lament the points when we don't appear to be getting further forward toward our originally declared destination and wonder how we can (in that colloquially common way) 'get back on track'.

In every instance we are propelled by the actions of our writing and manner by which our individual creativity encourages us to navigate and adventure and assess and confirm and step forward in our artistic use of written language. That is what drives so many of us creative writers to want to write, even when our journey is difficult and even more when we are uncertain where and when we will arrive. We venture out, and we take on the challenges, because we seek to make discoveries, and often to share with others the discoveries we make.

References

Arms, William Y., *Digital Libraries*, Boston: The MIT Press, 2000 (Last Accessed, August 30, 2023). https://archive.org/details/digitallibraries0000arms_j3c7

Hofmann, Gert and Snježana Zorić, *Topodynamics of Arrival: Essays on Self and Pilgrimage*, Amsterdam: Brill, 2012.

Runco, Mark A. and Garrett J. Jaeger, 'Standard Definition of Creativity', *Creativity Research Journal*, 24, no. 1, 2012, pp. 92–96.

BIBLIOGRAPHY

Albee, Edward in Digby Diehl, 'Edward Albee: An Interview', *The Transatlantic Review*, 48, no. 13, Summer 1963.

Allen, Graham, 'Shelley as Visual Artist: Doodles, Sketches, Ink Blots, and the Critical Reception of the Visual', *Studies in Romanticism*, 60, no. 3, 2021, pp. 277–306.

Arms, William Y., *Digital Libraries*, Boston: The MIT Press, 2000 (Last Accessed, August 30, 2023).

Baron, Nick, *Maps and the 20th Century: Drawing the Line*, Tom Harper (ed), London: British Library, 2016.

Barratt-Pugh, Caroline, Amelia Ruscoe and Janet Fellowes, 'Motivation to Write: Conversations with Emergent Writers', *Early Childhood Education Journal*, 49, 2021, pp. 223–234.

Beghetto, Ronald A., Maciej Karwowski and Roni Reiter-Palmon, 'Intellectual Risk Taking: A Moderating Link Between Creative Confidence and Creative Behavior?', *Psychology of Aesthetics, Creativity, and the Arts*, 15, no. 4, 2021, pp. 637–644.

Borel, Émile, 'La mécanique statique et l'irréversibilité' ('Statistical Mechanics and Irreversibility'), *Journal of Physics: Theories and Application*, 3, no. 1, 1913, pp. 189–196.

Bouchard, Jennifer, *Introduction to Literary Context: American Poetry of the 20th Century*, Hackensack, NJ: Salem Press, 2014.

Brady, Tara, https://www.dailymail.co.uk/news/article-2326630/Notes-diagrams-famous-authors-including-J-K-Rowling-Sylvia-Plath-planned-novels.html (Last Accessed, December 22, 2023).

Britannia Dictionary, https://www.britannica.com/dictionary/start (Last Accessed, January 2, 2024).

Brodsky, Joseph, 'Aesthetics and Language', in *Nobel Prize Lectures: From the Literature Laureates, 1986–2006*, Nobel Foundation, New York: New Press, 2007, p.255–267.

Bullard, Edward Crisp, 'The Magnetic Field within the Earth', *Proceedings of the Royal Society of London. Series A, Mathematical and Physical Sciences*, 197, no. 1051, July 7, 1949, pp. 433–453.

Burroughs, William in Eric Mottram, *William Burroughs: The Algebra of Need*, 1971, London: Marion Boyars, 1977.

Burroughs, William, *Junkie*, New York: Ace Books, 1953.

Burroughs, William, *Naked Lunch*, New York: Grove, 1959.

Buzan, Tony, *The Mind Map Book*, London: BBC Books, 1993.

Byars, Betsy, *Children's Books and Their Creators*, Anita Silvey (ed), Boston, MA: Houghton Mifflin, 1995.

Cameron, James, *The Terminator*, Los Angeles: Hemdale Pacific Western Productions, 1984.

Canales, Jimena, *The Physicist and the Philosopher: Einstein, Bergon and the Debate that Changed the Understanding of Time*, Princeton: Princeton University Press, 2016.

Carter, Rita, *Mapping the Mind*, London: Weidenfeld and Nicholson, 1998.

Clegg, Brian, *Ten Patterns That Explain the Universe*, Boston: MIT Press, 2021.

Collins English Dictionary, https://www.collinsdictionary.com/us/dictionary/english/start (Last Accessed, November 1, 2023).

Cummings, E. E., *ViVa*, New York: Liverright, 1997 (first published 1931).

Deleuze, Gilles and Felix Guattari, *A Thousand Plateaus: Capitalism and Schizophrenia*, trans. Brian Massumi, London: The Athlone Press, 1987.

Doctorow, E, L., in Randi Henderson, '"Ragtime" to Riches: Non-writing Is Doctorow's Neurosis', *The Baltimore Sun*, March 31, 1981.

Doctorow, E. L., *Reporting the Universe* (William E. Massey, Sr., Lectures in the History of American Civilization), Boston: Harvard University Press, 2004.

Eliot, T.S., 'Preface', in *Transit of Venus*, Harry Crosby (ed), Paris: Black Sun Press, 1931, pp. viii–ix.

Emerson, Ralph Waldo, *The Complete Works of Ralph Waldo Emerson*, Cambridge, MA: Riverside Press, 1903.

Ferguson, Ronald F. and Tatsha Robertson, *The Formula: Unlocking the Secrets of Raising Highly Successful Children*, Dallas: BenBella Books, 2019.

Franzen, Jonathan, Louisiana Channel, https://channel.louisiana.dk/video/jonathan-franzen-facing-blank-page, 2016 (Last Accessed, January 5, 2024).

Franzen, Jonathan, *The Corrections*, New York: Farrar, Straus and Giroux, 2001.

Freud, Sigmund, 'Creative Writing and Daydreaming', in Ernest Jones Freud (ed), *Collected. Papers, Vol. 4*, London: Bask Books (Hogarth Press), 1953.

Frost, Robert, *A Boy's Will*, Nutt: London, 1913.

Frost, Robert, *North of Boston*, Nutt: London, 1914.

Frost, Robert, 'The Road Not Taken', in *The Oxford Book of American Verse*, Francis Otto Mathieson (ed), Oxford: Oxford University Press, 1950. Originally published 1915.

Frost, Robert, *The Letters of Robert Frost*, Donald Sheehy, Mark Richardson and Robert Faggen (eds), Cambridge: Belknap Press, 2014.

Gardner, John, *The Art of Fiction: Notes on Craft for Young Writers*, New York: Alfred A. Knopf, 1984.

George, Lynell, 'Patience, Practice, Perseverance, How Octavia E. Butler Became a Writer', *The American Scholar*, 92, no. 4, Autumn 2023, pp. 100–112.

Glück, Louise in William Giraldi, 'Internal Tapestries: A Q&A with Louise Glück', *Poets and Writers Magazine*, September/October 2014.

Grogan, Daniel, *Origins of a Journey: History's Greatest Adventures Marked by Ambition, Necessity and Madness*, Kennebunkport: Appleseed, 2020.

Gurney, Alan, *The Compass*, Norton: New York, 2004.

Harper, Graeme, *Critical Approaches to Creative Writing*, Abington: Routledge, 2019.

Harper, Graeme, *Creative Writing Analysis*, London: Routledge, 2023.

Heaney, Seamus, 'Digging', *Death of a Naturalist*, Boston: Faber and Faber, 1991 (first published 1966), pp. 1–2.

Heaney, Seamus, quoted in O'Driscoll D., 'Pickings and Choosings', *The Poetry Ireland Review*, no. 87, August 2006, pp. 113–119.

Hemingway, Sean, 'Introduction', in Ernest Hemingway (ed), *For Whom the Bells Tolls*, New York: Scribner, 2019, pp. XIII–XXIII.

Hofmann, Gert and Snježana Zorić, *Topodynamics of Arrival: Essays on Self and Pilgrimage*, Amsterdam: Brill, 2012.

Honan, Park, *Jane Austen: Her Life*, New York: Ballantine, 1987.

Hosseini, Khaled in Noah Charney, 'Khaled Hosseini: How I Write', *Daily Beast*, July 14, 2017, https://www.thedailybeast.com/khaled-hosseini-how-i-write (Last Accessed, January 5, 2024).

Johnson, Samuel, *Samuel Johnson's Dictionary*, https://johnsonsdictionaryonline.com/views/search.php?term=start (Last Accessed, December 22, 2023).

Kleppe, Bård, 'Theatres as Risk Societies: Performing Artists Balancing between Artistic and Economic Risk', *Poetics*, 64, 2017, pp. 53–62.

Kosinski, Jerzy in Plimpton, George A. and Rocco Landesman, 'The Art of Fiction XLVI: Jerzy Kosinski', *Paris Review*, 14, no. 54, Summer 1972, pp. 183–207.

Kovecses, Zoltan, *Metaphor: A Practical Introduction*, 2nd ed., Oxford: Oxford University Press, 2010.

Kubrick, Stanley, *2001: A Space Odyssey*, London: Stanley Kubrick Productions, 1968.

Lakoff, George and Mark Johnson, *Metaphors We Live By*, Chicago: University of Chicago Press, 1980.

Lopez, Lorraine, 'The Architecture of Story', in *A Companion to Creative Writing*, Graeme Harper (ed), Oxford: Blackwell, 2013, pp. 9–23.

Lubart, Todd, 'In Search of the Writer's Creative Process', in *The Psychology of Creative Writing*, Scott Barry Kaufman and James C. Kaufman (eds), Cambridge: Cambridge University Press, 2009, pp. 149–165.

Maass, Donald, *The Emotional Craft of Fiction: How to Write the Story Beneath the Surface*, New York: Writer's Digest Books, 2016.

Maibom, Heidi, *The Space Between: How Empathy Really Works*, New York: Oxford University Press, 2022.

Messud, Clare, 'Bard of the Bayou', *The Guardian*, September 20, 1997. https://www.theguardian.com/books/1997/sep/20/fiction.williamfaulkner (Last Accessed, January 4, 2024).

Munro, Alice in Jeanne McCulloch and Mona Simpson, 'The Art of Fiction No. 137', *Paris Review*, 36, no. 131, Summer 1994, pp. 226–264.

Murakami, Haruki, *Hear the Wind Sing*, Tokyo: Kodansha, 1979.

Murakami, Haruki, *Pinball, 1973*, Tokyo: Kodansha, 1980.

Murata, Sayaka, Louisiana Channel, https://channel.louisiana.dk/video/sayaka-murata-on-facing-the-blank-page, 2022 (Last Accessed, January 5, 2024).

Naipaul, V.S., 'Two Worlds', in *Nobel Prize Lectures: From the Literature Laureates, 1986–2006*, Nobel Foundation, New York: New Press, 2007. pp. 69–83.

O'Connor, Flannery, *The Habit of Being: Letters of Flannery O'Connor*, Sally Fitzgerald (ed), New York: Farrar, Straus and Giroux, 1979.

Oates, Joyce Carol, Louisiana Channel, https://channel.louisiana.dk/video/joyce-carol-oates-facing-blank-page, 2014 (Last Accessed, January 5, 2024).

Orwell, George, *Nineteen Eighty-Four*, London: Secker and Warburg, 1949.

Oxford English Dictionary, https://www.oed.com/dictionary/start_n2?tab=meaning_and_use#20875761 (Last Accessed, January 2, 2024).

Pinheiro, Sylvia, Natalia Bezerra Mota, Mariano Sigmanc, Diego Femandez-Slezal, Antonio Guerreiro, Lufs Fernando Tófoli, Guillermo Cecchii, Mauro Copellii and Sidarta Ribeiro, 'The History of Writing Reflects the Effects of Education on Discourse Structure: Implications for Literacy, Orality, Psychosis and the Axial Age', *Trends in Neuroscience and Education*, 21, 2020, p. 100142.

Power, Arthur, *Conversations with James Joyce*, Clive Hart (ed), London: Millington, 1974.

Ricoeur, Paul, *The Rule of Metaphor*, London: Routledge & Kegan Paul, 1978.

Runco, Mark A. and Garrett J. Jaeger, 'Standard Definition of Creativity', *Creativity Research Journal*, 24, no. 1, 2012, pp. 92–96.

Schmandt-Besserat, Denise, 'Writing, Evolution of', in *International Encyclopedia of the Social & Behavioral Sciences*, 2nd ed., James D. Wright (ed), Oxford: Elsevier, 2015, pp. 761–766.

Sniezek, Janet A., 'Decision Making', in *Adolescent Health and Wellness*, Paul Moglia (ed), Ipswich: Grey House, 2015, pp. 908–911.

Song, Celine in Scott Feinberg, 'I Want to Do More Than Drive the Plot Forward', *Hollywood Reporter*, 429, no. 34, 2023, pp. 80–85.

Steinbeck, John in George Plimpton and Frank Crowther, 'The Art of Fiction No. 45', *Paris Review*, 16, no. 63, Fall 1975, pp. 180–194.

Stevens, Walter, *How Writing Made Us Human, 3000 BC to Now*, Baltimore: Johns Hopkins University Press, 2023.

Wasserman, Edward and Ralph Miller, 'Elementary Associative Learning', *Annual Review of Psychology*, 48, 1997, pp. 573–607.

Webster, Noah, *American Dictionary of the English Language*, 1828, https://webstersdictionary1828.com/Dictionary/start (Last Accessed, January 2, 2024).

Whedon, Joss, *Avengers: Age of Ultron*, Burbank: Marvel Studios, 2015.

INDEX

Printed and bound by CPI Group (UK) Ltd, Croydon, CR0 4YY

13/08/2024

01025821-0017